Chinese

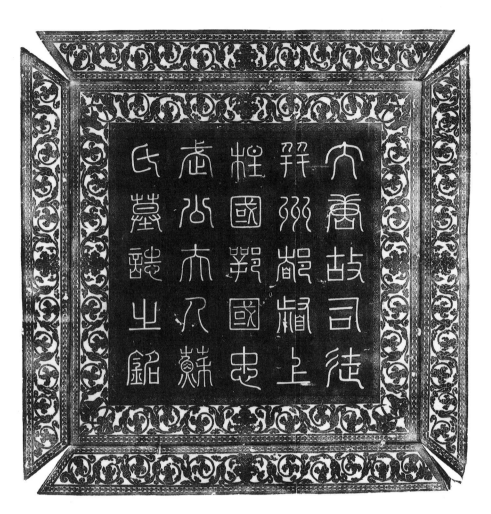

Rubbing from the stone epitaph cover made in AD 659 for the noblewoman
Su Wu (589–613), L. of edge 99 cm, stone located Zhaoling Museum, Liquan
county, Shaanxi province, rubbing coll. BM (OA) 1997.2-7.124.

Chinese

Oliver Moore

Published for The Trustees of

The British Museum by

BRITISH MUSEUM ⛪ PRESS

Acknowledgements

For invaluable advice and practical help I am deeply obliged to Robert Bagley, John Banks, Gilles Béguin, David Bellamy, William Boltz, Chang Suxia, Chen Lie, Paul van Dongen, Peter Engelfriet, Anne Farrer, Irving Finkel, Antoine Gournay, Jessica Harrison-Hall, Robert Knox, Elizabeth Lambourn, Matsumaru Michio, Meng Fanfeng, Carol Michaelson, Momiyama Akira, Ngo Tak Wing, Stephen Quirke, Jessica Rawson, Andrew Robinson, Sato Masayuki, Ivo Smits, Sun Ji, Tomiya Itaru, Helen Wang, Wang Tao, Clio Whittaker, Jeroen Wiedenhof and Zhao Chao. For the photographs I must thank Kevin Lovelock and John Williams of the British Museum Photographic Service. I am grateful to Chan Hing Wan who wrote the characters. I owe a special debt to Nina Shandloff, the editor, Jemima Scott-Holland, picture researcher, and John Hawkins, the designer.

Transcription of Chinese Pronunciation

Unless otherwise indicated, the transcription used throughout this book is *pinyin*, the standard system of writing Standard Modern Chinese with the Roman alphabet in the People's Republic of China since 1958. This has largely replaced the Wade-Giles system that was used in most English publications. The reader's attention is drawn to a few special uses of consonants:

Pinyin	Wade-Giles	English equivalent
c	ts'	lo*ts*
z	ts	loa*ds*
zh	ch	*j*oke
q	ch'	*ch*oke
x	hs	between s*ing* and *sh*ingle

Where a character possesses two readings, and in cases where a second character stands for a first, the alternatives are indicated by an oblique (/).

Oliver Moore has asserted his right to be identified as the Author of this work.

A catalogue record for this book is available from the British Library

ISBN 0–7141–8079–3

Designed and set in Sabon by John Hawkins Book Design
Printed in Great Britain by The Bath Press, Avon

Contents

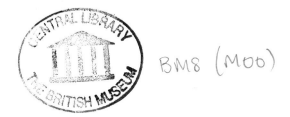
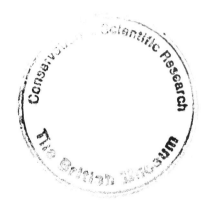

Preface

Any account of reading the Chinese past is enriched by the fact that Chinese writing is both ancient and current. No other writing system of antiquity enjoys this benefit.

This book defines the Chinese language both as a member of an East Asian language family and as a broad term covering quite distinct variations in speech within the borders of modern China (ch. 1). It then discusses how the Chinese writing system works today (ch. 2) before providing an account of evidence for the origins of Chinese writing in 1200 BC and its later developments (chs 3–5). Most of this discussion is devoted to the history of writing as far as the third century BC (chs 3–4). These centuries cover the formative stage in the development of a writing system. Thus, disregarding questions of style, by the dawn of China's imperial history most scholars and scribes were keen to define right and wrong ways to write Chinese characters. Conversely, the following centuries offer much less to any understanding of the development of the writing system, but they are of major interest in the continuing story of stylistic adaptations in calligraphy, arguably China's foremost cultural pursuit (ch. 5). Finally, Chinese writing has exerted its influence far beyond the traditional borders of China. The last chapter of this book illustrates instances of Chinese characters borrowed to write non-Chinese languages.

The book includes examples that may interest museum-goers who notice that Chinese artefacts often bear inscriptions and wish to know what those inscriptions state. The purpose of these examples is also to demonstrate some of the methods used to decipher ancient texts whose characters and their meanings are not always instantly clear. The aim here is to provide a selective overview of changes in form and style that writing underwent during China's long history and in different areas of her vast geography. This short account omits many details, but most are treated at length in the sources listed under Further Reading.

1
Languages in China

More people speak a Chinese language than any other. Chinese is the means of communication for nearly a billion people in China, as well as considerable numbers in Chinese communities overseas, and its system of writing is the most influential in East Asia. The notion of a single Chinese language, however, is deceptive. Despite several long periods under unified rule during which conscious efforts were made to impose uniformity of language and expression, China still remains home to several related but highly distinct forms of spoken Chinese. This fact is seldom sufficiently understood outside China, particularly since the Chinese writing system is often assumed to represent a linguistic homogeneity from one end of the country to the other.

Chinese – comprising all the variations shown on the map in fig. 1.1 – is a member of the Sino-Tibetan family of languages, which comprises two sub-families, Sinitic and Tibeto-Burman. Chinese belongs to the Sinitic sub-family, as do several tribal languages of south China, although their affiliation to this sub-family is still somewhat hypothetical. Spoken Chinese is not related to either Japanese or Korean, whose origins, much debated, may be linked to the Altaic family. Vietnamese languages, another major group, belong to the Mon-Khmer sub-family of Austro-Asiatic languages. Despite its separate family membership, however, Chinese writing has been highly influential in the development of the writing systems used in Korea, Japan and Vietnam.

Language and Dialect

We know very little of speech and speech variations within the society that first used a writing system ancestral to the Chinese writing system of today. The origins of writing in China are located in the Yellow River valley in north China (see ch. 3), but the furthest extent of these valley-dwellers' language usage is not precisely known. However, whatever area these limits once enclosed *c.* 1200 BC, it would have been dramatically smaller than the territory displayed in fig. 1.1.

Today, the distinct forms of speech used by sizeable groups of Chinese people in China and overseas are often called 'dialects'. The Chinese form is *fangyan*, 'regional languages'. Use of the term 'dialects' usually obscures the fact, however, that the various forms of speech covered by the large zones in fig. 1.1, and even

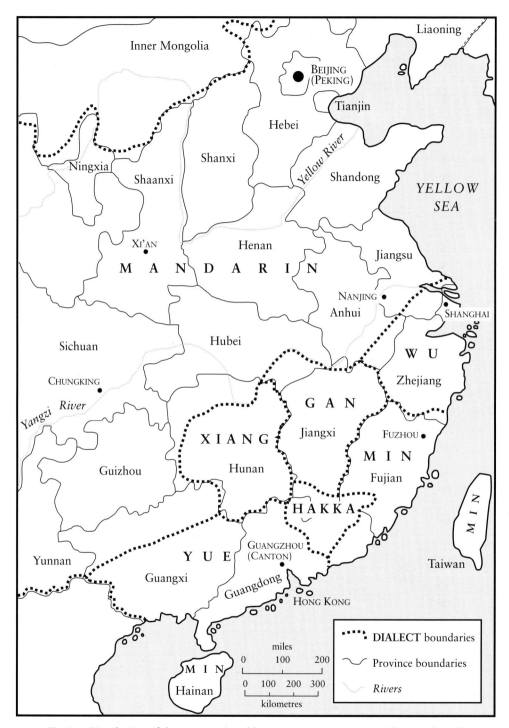

Fig. 1.1 Distribution of the major regional languages in contemporary China. Adapted from S. Robert Ramsey, *The Languages of China*, Princeton, NJ, 1987: fig. 6.

some of the speech varieties within those zones, are more often than not mutually unintelligible.

Even in China, efforts over many centuries to impose unifying cultural standards over a vast territory have often resulted in large language differences being minimized conceptually as variations of dialect.

Chinese Language Areas

The map (fig. 1.1) shows seven principal areas of Chinese speech. A basic division is drawn along the lower course of the Yangzi River. The language areas of the south are named after the principal rivers (Xiang and Gan) or after the historical names (Min and Yue) of people in these regions. Wu is the name of an ancient kingdom. Hakka – or Kejia – is a name meaning 'guest people', and signifies the northern origins of this large group of speakers who centuries ago migrated southwards. However, these names are primarily for academic or literary use. Most commonly, people in China refer to languages or dialects by the names of provinces, cities or towns where they are spoken, providing such familiar English names as Cantonese and Shanghainese.

The southern languages taken together are spoken by some thirty per cent of the entire Chinese population. The Wu language alone is spoken by more than eighty million people, a number equivalent to the population of Germany. Speakers of the Yue (Cantonese) dialects number nearly forty-eight million (excluding overseas communities), more than the population of Spain. Although obvious links between these Chinese languages exist, they differ considerably in their pronunciation, syntactical features and many basic items of vocabulary.

Standard Modern Chinese

China's official language today has several names, of which a familiar one outside China is Mandarin. The term Mandarin is probably derived from *mantri*, a Hindi word descended from the Sanskrit for 'counsellor', which early Portuguese voyagers to the Malay peninsula rendered as *mandarim*. Europeans used this name during the Renaissance to describe the officials who governed the Chinese empire as well as their language, which was the speech of courtly and official interaction. It was a standardized form of northern speech, represented particularly by the language of Beijing, and its status as an official language received its first great impetus with the establishment of Yanjing (modern Beijing) as a northern seat of government during the tenth century AD. The twentieth century has seen the introduction of terms such as 'national language' (*guoyu*) and – now current in mainland China – 'common speech' (*putonghua*). A Western equivalent now increasingly used is Standard Modern Chinese (SMC). Even though it belies historical accuracy, all the characters and texts referred to in the following pages are transcribed into SMC. The *pinyin* transcription system is described briefly at the beginning of this book.

Northern Chinese and related forms of speech that can be closely affiliated with SMC are used by about seventy per cent of the population, spread geographically in a diagonal swathe from the north-east to the south-west. Despite their political status, SMC and its ancestral languages have never been spoken by the entire population of China as a single native language. SMC today is simply the designated standard of speech throughout the whole country, and it is used with most consistency in government, education and the media. China remains home to several different Chinese languages, and a sizeable proportion of the population speaks SMC as a second language.

2
The Chinese Writing System

Chinese characters are made up of groups of strokes that fit into a notional square. In modern print it is easy to perceive the evenly sized space that each character occupies. Texts today are usually written horizontally towards the right, but short texts, such as the names on the outsides of buildings, are sometimes written horizontally and leftwards. Alternatively, texts can be written vertically towards the left – the traditional arrangement. Chinese newspapers can be typeset to be read horizontally or vertically on different areas of a page (fig. 2.1).

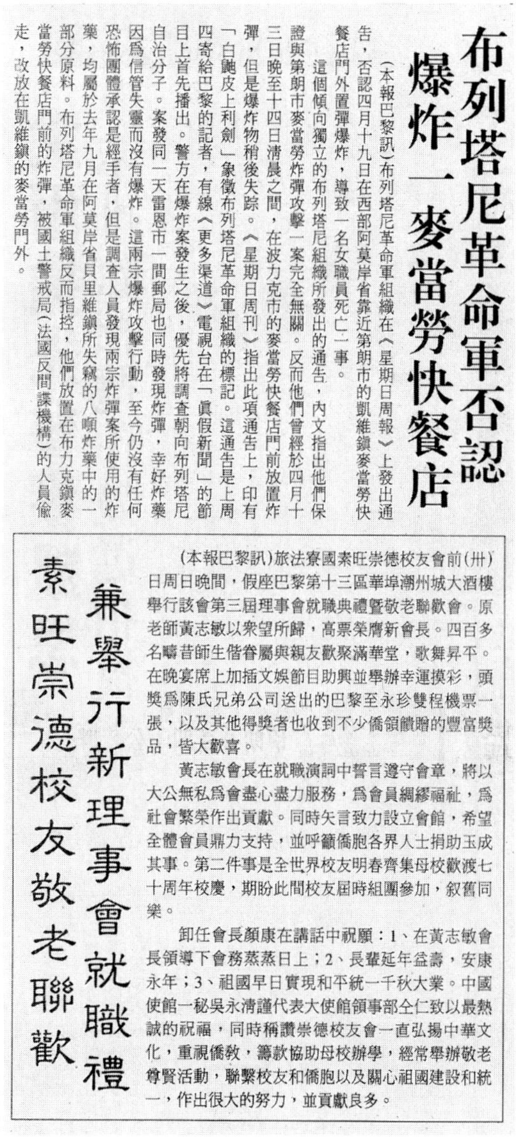

Fig. 2.1 Vertical and horizontal layouts of Chinese newsprint.

11

Units of Sound

Each character represents a single unit of sound, comprising either single or combined vowels or combinations of consonants and vowels. For example, in SMC:

Vowel	*e*	餓	'starve'
Vowels	*ao*	奧	'profound'
Consonant + vowel	*ba*	八	'eight'
Consonant + vowel + consonant	*ban*	版	'plank'

Regardless of whether such sounds consist of a single vowel or a combination of consonants and a vowel, they are written with one character. Each character conveys both sound and meaning.

Building words

Most commonly named a 'character', each unit can also be called a 'logogram', a term describing a writing system such as Chinese in which one symbol is used to write one word. This differs from an alphabetic system, in which symbols have evolved that are combined to signify a word by its constituent sounds. A logogram represents a word in terms of both sound and meaning, and the changing roles of a logogram in different circumstances of grammar and syntax alter neither the way it is written nor, except in rare cases, the way it is pronounced. Compare the Chinese sentences:

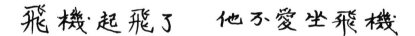

feiji qifei le　　　　　　　　*ta bu ai zuo feiji*
'The aeroplane took off'　　'He does not like taking aeroplanes'

The two logograms united to form both 'aeroplane' and 'aeroplanes' (*fei* 'fly' and *ji* 'mechanism') are not in any way modified to indicate either singular or plural use or their changing case as subject and object. The logogram *fei* 'to fly', used for the compound verb *qifei*, literally, 'arise and fly' ('to take off'), is indistinguishable from its appearance as part of a noun. This is quite distinct from Indo-European languages, in which nouns, adjectives and verbs change form and pronunciation – that is, are 'inflected' – according to the various grammatical roles they perform in a sentence. Russian, for instance, is a heavily inflected language whereas English is less so. Chinese words are not inflected at all.

SMC and other Chinese languages are often described as 'monosyllabic', a term that, however imperfectly, characterizes the isolated sound values of individual characters and also reflects the existence of a large number of single logograms – those words comprising only one sound unit represented by a single character. For example, *di* 'ground', *tian* 'sky', *ban* 'plank' and *shu* 'book' are all common monosyllabic items from the vocabulary of SMC. It would be misleading, however, to give the impression that all Chinese words are monosyllables represented by single characters. In fact, most Chinese words today are formed from two characters, like *feiji* above, and the evidence of ancient texts is that other two-character words such as *hudie* 'butterfly' have existed for two millennia or longer.

The concept of syllables is not readily applicable to Chinese words. No single word can be broken down into syllabic components, such as 'aer-o-plane', and a word formed of two characters, such as *feiji*, is not in any strict sense a polysyllabic compound, but rather a conjunction of the two units *fei* and *ji*.

Tonal distinctions

The range of sounds in SMC is quite limited, as are the distinct phonetic ranges of Shanghainese, Cantonese and other Chinese languages. This means that in any given language area many words share the same basic pronunciation. In SMC the following words are all pronounced *yang*:

狹	羊	仰	样
yāng	*yáng*	*yǎng*	*yàng*
'disaster'	'sheep'	'raise one's head'	'sample'

But, to the ear, each of these pronunciations is distinguished by its tone. Every sound in the language is pronounced with a particular tone. The example above shows *yang* pronounced variously with a level, rising, dipping or falling tone. Tones have developed over many centuries and, in the process, they have supplanted extra distinctions once heard in the form of final consonants. (Cantonese still has a relatively rich range of final consonants, but SMC retains only the closely related endings -*n* and -*ng*.) Tones are essential to spoken Chinese, and most children acquiring a Chinese language grasp the tones of words even before they can perfect their pronunciation.

The number of tones in the languages of southern China is generally higher, but SMC is restricted to four tones, each of which is exemplified in the last example. They are often simply denoted in dictionaries as one to four. Despite the distinctions offered by tones, however, ambiguities still remain. The following four characters are all pronounced *yang* in the second (rising) tone:

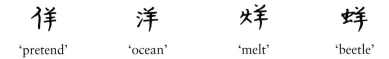

佯	洋	烊	蛘
'pretend'	'ocean'	'melt'	'beetle'

Two or more words sharing exactly the same pronunciation and tone are termed homophones. Of course, context alone generally prevents ambiguity, but situations where one or perhaps each participant in a dialogue has a weak grasp of the sounds of SMC, for example, may give rise to enormous confusion. Nor is this confusion solely a modern problem. Historical anecdotes could be adduced to illustrate both grievous and hilarious mismatches of sound and meaning over many centuries. In fact, such confusion has been the basis of a witty theatrical art invented long ago and still hugely popular today.

In writing, however, the ambiguity caused by the high incidence of homophones is absent. The process by which this is achieved reveals precisely the operation of the writing system today as well as its historical development.

Sound and Meaning in Characters

In theory at least, it might be possible to write all four words from the last example using the same character for 'sheep', employed solely for its phonetic value *yang*, since context would clarify the meaning. Indeed, the verbs 'pretend' and 'melt' would occur only in positions appropriate for a verb, and other details of context would make a choice between the two words even more obvious. This theoretical possibility would offer a significant step towards phonetic writing, that is the use of symbols to represent only the sounds of words. But it would remain impossible to render entirely unambiguous the meanings of words that share the same sound. Thus, four words all pronounced *yang* had to be graphically distinguishable from one another.

The four characters may be analysed as combinations of two elements: sound and meaning. The pronunciation *yang* is shown as the right-hand element of all four characters. This element is called a phonetic, since it signifies a sound and tells the reader how to pronounce the word. Each word's general area of meaning is given in the left-hand side. This element of the character's composition is called the determinative. The second character, for instance, uses the 'water' determinative in the word for 'ocean'. Thus the reader who already knows that the word for ocean is *yang* will encounter a character that bears the phonetic for *yang* and includes the determinative associating it with water. Readers who encounter this character and recognize its pronunciation but not its meaning can use one of two methods to look it up. In a dictionary organized by pronunciations

the character will be located with all the others pronounced *yang* in the seco
tone. An alternative arrangement is to group all the entries under determinativ
so that the character in this case will be placed within a list of characters shari
the 'water' determinative.

The phonetic in the four words of this example, if written alone, is in fact the character for *yang* 'sheep'. It need hardly be argued that oceans, beetles, pretending and melting have no conceivable link with notions of sheep. The use of this particular character as a phonetic is determined purely by its function as signifier of the word's pronunciation as *yang* in the second tone.

Chinese writing early on developed logograms that combine a phonetic element with a semantic determinative (sometimes called a 'radical'). Today the majority of characters can be analysed as separable combinations of sound and meaning. Determinatives classify a character – and the word it represents – within a broad or sometimes quite narrow area of meaning. Thus, the determinatives for 'pretend', 'ocean', 'melt' and 'beetle' are those for 'man', 'water', 'fire' and 'insect'. These four determinatives appear on the left, but they can also appear at other positions in different characters. For example, the 'fire' determinative occupies the bottom of the word *zhu*, 'to boil':

The upper part of this character is the phonetic *zhu*. Determinatives appear at the top, bottom, left or right of a character, in positions that had become largely standardized by the end of the first millennium BC.

Characters as pictographs

A common description of Chinese characters is that they are pictures of things. It is true that a certain number of early characters and even their modern forms today are strongly representational depictions of what they name. Thus they are pictographic, but each communicates a precise meaning only as long as the reader has been instructed to recognize exactly what they depict. The following five characters depict, respectively, droplets of water descending from the sky; a crescent moon; a large-headed infant with outstretched arms; an eye and a halberd:

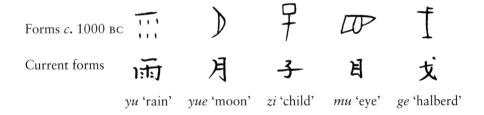

Forms *c.* 1000 BC

Current forms

yu 'rain'   *yue* 'moon'   *zi* 'child'   *mu* 'eye'   *ge* 'halberd'

The crucial concession is that the reader has been instructed. Otherwise, the 'moon' character could stand for a canoe, a fruit and many other plausible meanings. Such shifting possibilities could not sustain a writing system.

In the early development of Chinese writing a large number of characters were created with pictographic signs like the five examples above. And, with an awareness of how the concrete can depict the abstract, even words for the least visible notions could be written with characters that depicted tangible things. For instance, the word *zhong* 'finish' was written with a character that shows suspended ends of silk strands:

Still, an infinite generation of pictographic characters for every word in the language would be beyond the scope of even exceptional human ingenuity. Although there are many pictographic characters among the commonest lexical items of today's usage, the overwhelming majority of Chinese characters are now formed by a combination of phonetics and determinatives as described above.

Multivalence

The most significant step in developing a writing system must have been the realization that the character standing for one word could be used to write another word that shared the same sounds. The particular usage of characters that resulted from this realization is called multivalence, and it underlies much of the history of Chinese writing.

The earlier example of four distinct words all pronounced *yang* and all sharing the phonetic element for that pronunciation is an instance of multivalence. This example, however, represents a degree of organization that was never rigorously applied for at least the first thousand years of the development of writing in China. By contrast, what several texts in the following chapters will show is that early writing consistently used the character of one word to write a second word without adding a determinative to distinguish the two usages. The broad pattern of development in early writing was an evolution from the interchangeable usage of characters to write words with the same sounds towards the higher degrees of precision by which determinatives render unambiguous the meanings of homophones written with the same phonetic elements.

One of the most important strategies needed to interpret ancient texts is the fullest possible awareness of multivalent usages. The character *li* (shown on the cover of this book) once had the meaning 'tears':

The character is highly pictographic in the sense that it shows an eye above cascades of water. But it is used in this particular text to represent the conjunction *li* 'with', which does not have the remotest association with weeping and shares only the word's pronunciation. Context is the only determinant of the two meanings.

As the use of writing extended over increasing distances, the multivalence of characters was affected by distinct regional pronunciations. The resulting problem was that scribes in different regions – or even scribes in the same region – would write the same characters with a wide variety of phonetics, according to whatever sounded most suitable to their differently attuned ears. Practices for selecting determinatives frequently differed too. The problem would still exist today were it not for the fact that the sole accepted standard for the phonetic basis of Chinese writing is now SMC. However, this does not prevent writers of Chinese from inventing written forms for millions of dialect expressions that do not exist in SMC, and these inventions are then circulated through humorous columns, popular fiction and private communication.

Sometimes the historical conditions of multivalent usage make the interpretation of ancient texts very difficult indeed. But success is due in no small part to the continued use of Chinese characters over three millennia. This continuity is essential to enabling the earliest writings discovered in China to communicate messages to the modern world.

3
Early Evidence in
Divination Texts

Neolithic Marks

On present evidence it seems unlikely that writing was invented in China before or during the Neolithic (*c.* 6000–*c.* 1700 BC). Claims have, however, been made for such early origins. Pottery vessels discovered at several significantly advanced Neolithic sites bear incised marks, and several dozen marks have been collected from widely distributed sites. However, these are marks that existed singly – and some as pairs of marks – on individual ceramic vessels. They could have been ownership marks. But, as found, none can be combined with others as a text, and their wide distribution makes them an awkward sort of evidence.

A few marks show tantalizing similarities to the characters of what had become a flourishing writing system by 1200 BC. For instance, the pattern of four intersecting lines on the base of a grey jar unearthed in Jinshan county near Shanghai (fig. 3.1) is strikingly similar to the character for the name Xing as it appears *c.* 1000 BC (shown on the cover of this book and discussed in ch. 4).

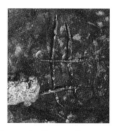

The character *xing c.* 1000 BC

Fig. 3.1 Mark on the base of a ceramic jar, H. 19.6 cm, *c.* 2500 BC, excav. Shanghai. After Huang Xuanpei, et al., *Gems of Liangzhu Culture from the Shanghai Museum*, Hong Kong, 1992: 144.

This object belonged to the Liangzhu culture, artistically one of the most sophisticated and productive East Coast cultures of the third millennium BC. The similarity is intriguing, but there is no evidence to show that the mark on it can be integrated within a sequence of other such marks, representing writing. It is one mark on one piece of pottery. Both this Neolithic mark and the character it closely resembles are simple combinations of lines, so that the probability of their chance resemblance is high. By contrast, sequences of several Neolithic marks, each consisting of, say, ten lines, dots and other features resembling characters of a later period, really would present a demanding challenge to commonly accepted ideas about when writing first appeared in China. At present, the most that can be said for Neolithic origins is that certain habits of drawing, patterning and combining elements in Neolithic pottery marks might have endured for many centuries before they provided some sort of basis for the first invention of writing signs. But this is highly speculative.

Archaeology has now revealed several highly organized states that existed *c.* 1200 BC in different zones of what is now China. Among them, the Shang state in north central China (*c.* 1500–1045 BC) has dominated views of the period as a result of brief mentions of its existence in much later historical records. In the twentieth century the discovery and interpretation of Shang inscriptions further boosted its historical pre-eminence. The Shang's development of a writing system seems to have been unique, and no investigation at other Bronze Age sites – or late Neolithic sites – in China can dispute this distinctive achievement.

China's earliest true writing emerged within the Shang state in or shortly before 1200 BC, and texts have survived on two principal media: oracle bones (discussed in this chapter) and bronze implements (discussed in the following chapter). A few pieces of inscribed pottery, stone, deer antler and even some fragments of human skull have also survived. Writing in this early period was probably also done on more perishable materials, such as wood or textiles, but no evidence has been found.

Divination Texts

The largest surviving body of writing from the Shang period comprises inscriptions on animal bones or reptile shells. These so-called 'oracle bones' were used to record divinations for the last kings of the Shang dynasty during the final 150 years of Shang power, that is *c.* 1200–1045 BC. In addition, Shang foundries cast bronze vessels and weapons, some of which bear short inscriptions. Surviving bronze objects and oracle bones were made and used during the same period, so it is somewhat artificial to adopt a chronological division in discussing them. However, whereas the practice of inscribing oracle bones declined soon after the overthrow of the Shang, inscribed vessels were produced for many centuries afterwards and so provided a much longer continuity for the early development of writing.

The discovery of oracle bones

Unknown to most of the outside world, farmers digging the land in Anyang county in Henan province during the nineteenth century often shovelled up extremely old mammal bones and turtle shells, which they called 'dragon bones'. Since the soil around Anyang had preserved these remains in a fragmented but relatively consistent condition, the diggers were able to sell their finds by weight to city-dwelling apothecaries or their agents. The bones were ground into powder and prescribed with other ingredients as drugs, and, by the close of the Qing dynasty (1644–1911), 'dragon bones' supplied a highly lucrative branch of traditional medicine.

A frequently related story describes how in 1899 Wang Yirong (1845–1900), one of the last directors of the Imperial Academy of State Education in Beijing, contracted malaria. The recommended cure for his condition included a quantity of 'dragon bones', which were duly sent to him (as yet unground) by one of the capital's leading pharmacies. It was a fortunate chance that both Wang and his house-guest at the time, Liu E (1857–1909), shared a strong interest in palaeography, and both men quickly realized that the marks on the pharmacy's bones were an early form of writing. Although they had limited success in reading what they saw, their momentous discovery inspired them – and later others – to collect as much inscribed material as possible. The bone trade boomed. Hitherto, paradoxically, bones with inscriptions on them had had no market value, and would-be sellers had scraped away the writing in order to make their finds saleable. After 1899, however, the situation was dramatically reversed.

An even more energetic pioneer of this period was the antiquary and philologist Luo Zhenyu (1866–1940) (fig. 3.2). Although bone dealers kept the true source of their trade a secret as long as possible, Luo Zhenyu extracted from them in 1908 the whereabouts of a site near Anyang, namely the village of Xiaotun. In 1915 he became the first collector-publisher to visit Xiaotun and actually see the place from which so much material had been exported.

In 1917 Luo Zhenyu's most gifted student, Wang Guowei (1877–1927), published his discovery that inscriptions on oracle bones proved that the list of Shang kings contained in the *Shiji* ('Historical Records'), completed early in the first century BC, was an accurate king-list. As well as a philological triumph, this was a discovery – or rediscovery – of huge cultural significance, proving that the transmitted texts of ancient Chinese history asserted verifiable facts. His triumph is tinged with irony, as it emerged at a time when some adherents of the nascent science of Chinese archaeology were trying to promote a more sceptical approach to the past than that provided by ancient scripture. In effect, Wang Guowei bolstered the increasingly controversial premise that the veracity of China's ancient scriptures should not be doubted.

During the large-scale official excavations at Anyang between 1928 and 1937 thousands more oracle bones were discovered. A concrete and visible gauge of the newness of these discoveries was the archaeologists' observation that grave diggers at Anyang in the sixth century AD had had to smash their way downwards

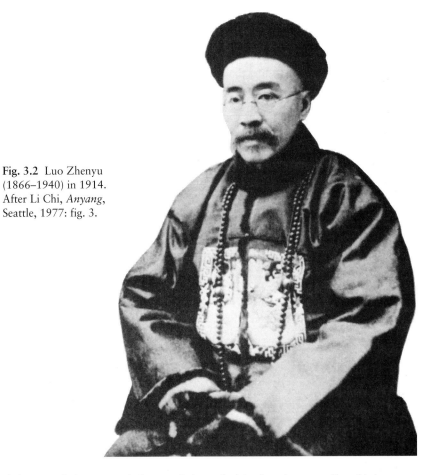

Fig. 3.2 Luo Zhenyu (1866–1940) in 1914. After Li Chi, *Anyang*, Seattle, 1977: fig. 3.

through layers of Shang oracle bones. It is probable that these medieval labourers might have scrutinized the bones at least cursorily before throwing them back with the earth infill for the tombs they had excavated. But, judging from what else we know of the period, it seems their chance discoveries led to no new insights concerning the origins of Chinese writing.

Excavations at Anyang continued at intervals throughout the century, and today the corpus of inscribed oracle bones totals approximately two hundred thousand. Most of these are in China and Taiwan, with less than 15 per cent in museums and libraries elsewhere in the world.

The divination process

Oracle bones were the means for divining the future. Two kinds of bone were used: an ox's shoulder blade (scapula) (fig. 3.3) and either a turtle's frontal plate (plastron) (fig. 3.4) or, less frequently, its dorsal shell (carapace).

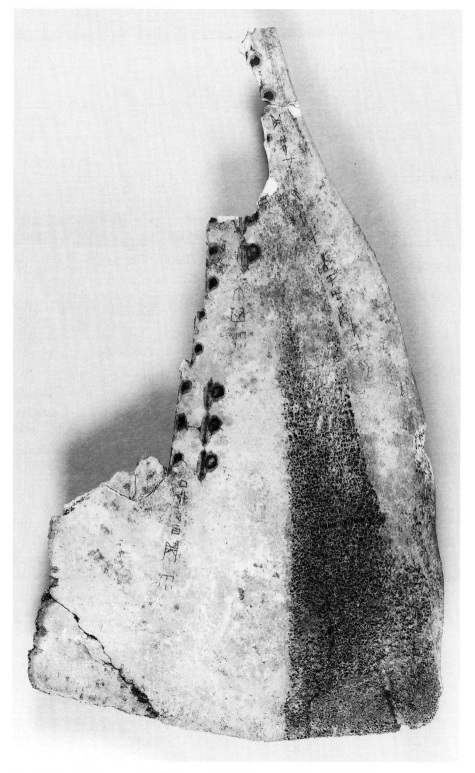

Fig. 3.3 Inscribed ox scapula, H. 30 cm, British Library, BL Or 7694.1987.

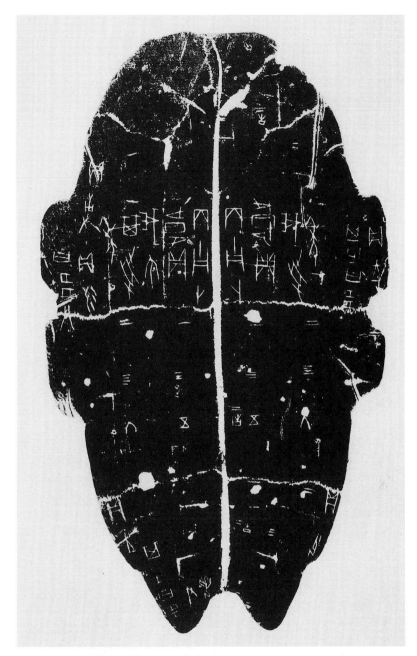

Fig. 3.4 Ink rubbing of an inscribed plastron, H. 19.8 cm, Academia Sinica, Taipei. After Shimonaka Kunihiko, ed., *Shodō zenshū*, vol. 1, Tokyo, 1954: fig. 1.

Bones and shells were trimmed, cleaned and even polished. The series of pits bored or cut into their concave undersides stopped just short of completely piercing the object. The photograph of a scapula in fig. 3.3 shows a column of three pits inside its left edge. Intense heat – probably a white-hot rod – was applied to the pits to create a crack on the opposite surface.

During a divination, the diviner would announce the subject to be divined in the form of affirmative and negative statements. The following example from the plastron shown in fig. 3.4 is shown in a horizontal rearrangement (in this and following examples, characters in the lower line or in the right-hand column are current forms):

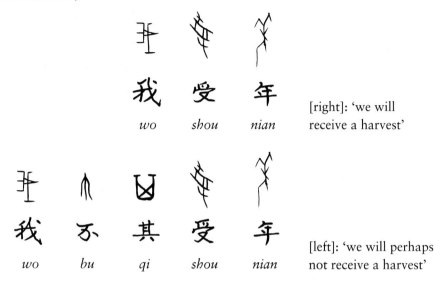

我 受 年
wo *shou* *nian*

[right]: 'we will receive a harvest'

我 不 其 受 年
wo *bu* *qi* *shou* *nian*

[left]: 'we will perhaps not receive a harvest'

It is difficult to measure what level of urgency statements like this betokened. If the previous years' harvests had been good, these simple statements could have been formal, recurrent expressions of royal power and control, supported by fair weather, abundant crops and a population of obedient farmers and slaves. If, however, this divination was phrased following three successive years of crop failure, its paired statements must have been symptoms of deep crisis. We might then imagine a Shang king desperate to salvage his state's economic base as well as to escape the growing prospect of mass starvation, internal uprisings, invasion by a strong neighbour or any of the other political nightmares that visited autocrats of the ancient world. Similar scenarios might be inferred from the inscriptions on the British Library's scapula (fig. 3.3), which concern the question of whether or not rain is imminent.

Diviners' statements like the above examples would have been pronounced aloud several times, but nothing would have been written on the bone until after the whole divining process had been concluded. Divining and inscribing were two separate activities. Following each alternative announcement of a positive and negative statement, the diviner scorched opposite halves of the bone. One half would have been nominated negative and the other positive. The bone would be examined afterwards to determine which crack in which half of the bone best revealed the coming direction of events.

Following these rituals, bones were inscribed to name the day of a particular divination, identify the diviner, number the cracks, record the diviner's statements and, less commonly, record the king's prognostication. Diviners did not inscribe the oracle bones themselves, but handed them over to inscribers. This division of tasks can be deduced from diverse writing styles in the records of divinations carried out by the same diviner. In other cases, it is clear that a unique writing style unifies texts associated with two or more diviners. Although our knowledge of these people's lives is severely limited, one fragment of an oracle bone records the intention to build a school within the Shang royal residence (fig. 3.5). Perhaps this establishment – if it was ever built – was created to train inscribers and diviners.

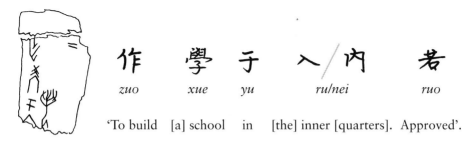

作　　學　　于　　入／內　　　若

zuo　　*xue*　　*yu*　　　*ru/nei*　　　　*ruo*

'To build　[a] school　in　[the] inner [quarters].　Approved'.

Fig. 3.5 Fragment of inscribed oracle bone, *c.* 1200 BC, coll. Institute of the Humanities, Kyoto University. Drawing after Li Pu, *Jiaguwen xuanzhu*, Shanghai, 1989: 240.

The arrangement and appearance of characters

The writing on oracle bones was cut into the bone surface with a sharp tool, but it is not unlikely that a draft was first marked on the bone surface in a pigment. A sherd of pottery dating to the Shang period and inscribed in ink with the word *si* 'sacrifice' provides important evidence that some form of ink and a brush were available during the Shang (fig. 3.6).

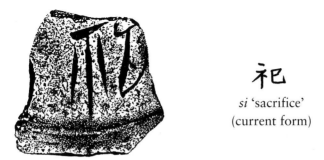

祀

si 'sacrifice'
(current form)

Fig. 3.6 Ceramic sherd inscribed with ink, *c.* 1200 BC, after Li Ji, *Xiaotun (Henan Anyang Yinxu yizhi zhi yi) di san ben – Yinxu qiwu, jia bian: taoqi – shang ji*, Nangang [Taiwan], 1956: pl. 22.

The cracks were numbered in the order in which they had been made. It is sometimes obvious that the longer texts of the diviner's statements were written around the zones occupied by the numbers, and, in a few cases, numbers were evidently erased to create more space. The numbers must therefore have been cut before writing the rest of the inscription. Numbers 1 to 6, which are the six characters transcribed below, can be seen on the lower portion of the plastron in fig. 3.4:

一	二	三	四	五	六
'one'	'two'	'three'	'four'	'five'	'six'

Affirmative statements were written on one side with their negations opposite. Vertical and horizontal arrangements of text were oriented either side of the vertical axis on shells, which is formed by the natural fissure running from gullet to rectum. The text in fig. 3.4 is particularly interesting, since it displays the first five characters of both statements – the two columns closest to the axis – as mirror images of each other:

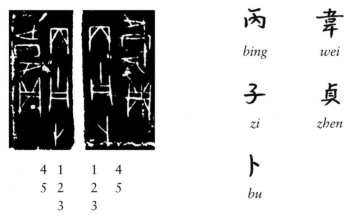

bing   wei

zi   zhen

bu

'*Bingzi* [day 13] cracks [made], Wei divined'

The internal compositions of the fourth character, the diviner's name, Wei, and the third character, *bu* 'to make cracks', mirror each other in precisely opposite directions. An exact standard in the orientation of a character's composition was evidently not yet a priority.

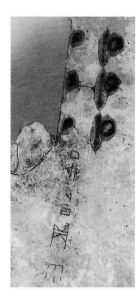

Reading Oracle Bone Texts

Texts on oracle bones are often (but not always) arranged with some degree of symmetry, as not all divinations consisted of positive and negative pairs of statements. Inscribers located different divinations within distinct zones on the same object, but they did not use any marks that might be considered punctuation in a modern sense. The positive statement precedes, so, for instance, the inscription on the scapula in fig. 3.3 (left) opens on the lower left:

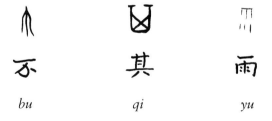

| ding | mao | bu | Xuan | zhen | yu |

'*Ding mao* [day 4], cracks [made], Xuan [name of diviner] divined: [it will] rain'.

The first two characters name the day using a cycle of sixty day-names (discussed below). The rest of the opening follows the common formula described above. The three characters of a negating statement are placed higher up to the right (below):

| bu | qi | yu |

'Perhaps not rain'

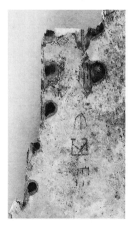

The literal order of these characters is: 'not – perhaps – rain'. Most of the characters of this inscription are relatively easy to identify on the basis of later forms and even their appearance today, as shown below:

Oracle bone	Bronze	Current forms
		不 *bu*
		其 *qi*
		雨 *yu*

The bottom character in the table above, *yu* 'rain', shows a close correspondence between the word's meaning and how the character depicts a thing or phenomenon – provided, of course, that all readers agree that the character in question shows droplets of water falling out of the sky. Even though such correspondences were still quite common at this stage in the history of writing, they cannot be taken for granted as a key with which to decipher oracle bone inscriptions. For instance, the character *qi*, second in the inscription on the scapula in fig. 3.3 and shown in the middle row of the table above, is an example of a phonetic loan. This character, here meaning 'perhaps', also stands for the word for 'basket', and its form suggests handles above the criss-cross weave of a container. The character as used in bronze inscriptions shows the same appearance although extra elements were often added beneath. The most common instance of this character in surviving inscriptions is as a phonetic borrowing, to write a grammatical particle that acts like an adverb or verb, indicating the probability of an event.

This propensity to borrow one character to write a second one sharing the same pronunciation presents interpretative difficulties, but it is crucial to understanding the development of the writing system. In the inscriptions on both the scapula and the plastron (figs 3.3 and 3.4), the fifth character is a verb now transcribed as *zhen* 'to divine'. This transcription follows the modern pronunciation of the verb, but this ahistorical convention obscures the workings of the Shang system of writing. The verb 'to divine' was written with a phonetic loan using a character which meant 'tripod vessel', now read *ding*. The oracle bone character is strongly suggestive of the object itself, showing a container above two of its three legs:

Reconstructing exactly how these words for a 'tripod vessel' and for 'divining' were pronounced in Shang times need not concern us closely; what is important is that they sounded the same or extremely similar. Because of this close similarity, the second word could be written with the character for the first. Significantly, to distinguish the use of the character for a word meaning 'to divine', some occurrences on oracle bones show a determinative in the form of *bu* 'to make cracks' at the top of the character:

Oracle bone form   Current form of *zhen*

What we see in the current form still includes the two strokes of *bu* 'to make cracks'. Its phonetic component, although once borrowed from the character for a tripod vessel, has been reduced and modified beyond recognition. Since the character in the oracle bone inscriptions stands for a word now pronounced *zhen*, conventional transcriptions adopt that pronunciation rather than the pronunciation *ding*. This is a logical choice, but its elimination of the sound *ding* obscures the phonetic principles underlying Shang writing, and ignores the essential point that one Chinese character could offer a phonetic value with which to write two words with distinct meanings.

Changes in writing during the late Shang

A vital factor in deciphering and dating the bones was the two initial characters of the opening formula, which were used for naming the days. No year-dates were written on oracle bones, as the day and month were of paramount concern to the people who used divination and created its written records. The Shang used a combination of two series of ten and twelve characters, and consecutively paired them to form a cycle of sixty named days. An equivalent based on the series A–J and 1–12 would be:

A	B	C	D	E	F	G	H	I	J	A	B	C	D	etc.
1	2	3	4	5	6	7	8	9	10	11	12	1	2	etc.

This sequence continues until the sixtieth combination (J12) permits a new beginning at A1. The so-called 'ten stems and twelve branches' sequence remained in use throughout subsequent history, and, as bronze inscriptions discussed in the following chapter show, the 'stems' were used to name ancestors by association with the days on which sacrificial observances to them were due. The sequence is still used today for the day order in the Chinese lunar calendar. Although the differences between Shang forms of these characters and their later equivalents are considerable, the ubiquity of day-dates in divination inscriptions makes it possible to observe major changes in written forms across the entire history of writing in the late Shang.

An emphatic example of these changes is the inscription on a bone in fig. 3.7. It is a text composed entirely of day-dates:

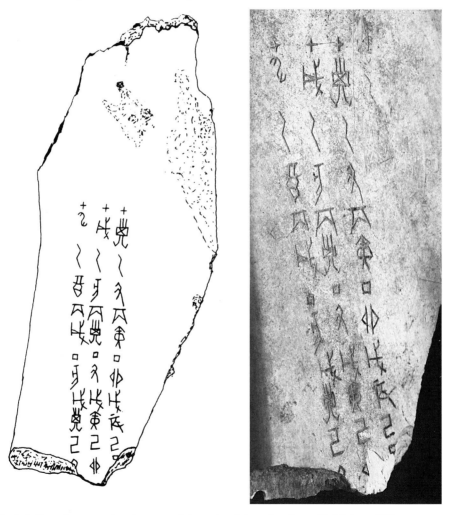

Fig. 3.7 Bone fragment showing part of the cycle of sixty day-dates, H. 14.4 cm, Rijksmuseum voor Volkenkunde, Leiden. After Jean A. Lefeuvre, *Several Collections of Oracular Inscriptions in Germany, Switzerland, the Netherlands, Belgium*, Taipei/Paris/San Francisco, 1997: 151–3.

Transcription and sequence:

[21] *jiashen* [A9]	[11] *jiaxu* [A11]	[1] *jiazi* [A1]
[22] *yiyou* [B10]	[12] *yihai* [B12]	[2] *yichou* [B2]
[23] *bingxu* [C11]	[13] *bingzi* [C1]	[3] *bingyin* [C3]
[24] *dinghai* [D12]	[14] *dingchou* [D2]	[4] *dingmao* [D4]
[25] *wuzi* [E1]	[15] *wuyin* [E3]	[5] *wuchen* [E5]
	[16] *jimao* [F4]	

This fragmentary text was not a divination record, and moreover there is no sign that the bone was ever burned. What the whole text once provided was a handy reference for ten-day intervals starting from any day in the whole sixty-day cycle. These intervals can be checked by selecting a particular day from the cycle of sixty and then reading leftwards across the row in which it stands. The top row of the inscription shows the combinations *jiazi*, *jiaxu* and *jiashen*, equivalent to A1, A11 and A9 (days 1, 11 and 21 respectively). Only five rows of this table survive. Presumably it once comprised ten rows of three combinations. Perhaps a second bone with the same arrangement of the remainder of the series (from day 31 onwards) was originally placed beside the one that has survived.

Apart from its interest as a calculating tool, this late Shang inscription is highly significant for the history of writing. The following comparison displays two characters of this text in the forms that they assumed at the beginning and the end of the late Shang period, referred to by historians and archaeologists as Periods I and V.

zi
(occurrences at 1, 13 and 25 in text of fig. 3.7)

yin
(occurrences at 3 and 15 in text of fig. 3.7)

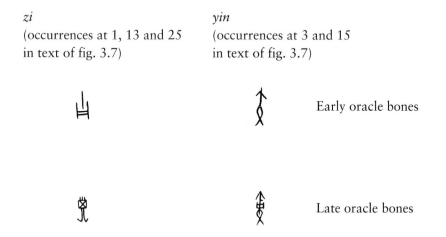

Early oracle bones

Late oracle bones

This table shows clearly that the inscription on the ox-bone (fig. 3.7) is a relic of Period V. The character *zi* in the combinations *jiazi*, *bingzi* and *wuzi* (1, 13, 25) on the bone, for instance, is tabulated as a form current during the late period.

Likewise, the characters *wu* and *yin* (appearing in the combinations for 5, 15, 25 and 3) are typical Period V forms.

The evidence of these chronological comparisons is significant. Characters over the five periods of oracle bone history grew more complicated. Rather than gaining more fluent and sparer forms, they often became by Period V considerably denser. This suggests a deeply conservative control of the development of Chinese writing even at this early date. But this control was certainly not enforceable in all contexts of writing. The earlier and less complex forms of these characters were retained in many contemporary bronze inscriptions, and bronze inscriptions were to offer a much longer line of development in the following period.

The forms of the characters on the bone in fig. 3.7 date the text as a late Shang inscription. This dating fits exactly with what we know about divinations during the close of the Shang, when the kings became almost exclusively preoccupied with the ten-day cycles of the sacrificial timetable as well as the avoidance of evil within a ten-day period.

The practice of inscribing oracle bones soon declined, but pyromantic divination did not die out completely. Excavations during recent work on the Yangzi dam have revealed drilled and burned plastrons of the Tang period (AD 618–907), and divination using plastrons and scapulae may still be observed in some regions of China and Taiwan today.

Even if the urge to record divinations vanished soon after the overthrow of the Shang by the Zhou in 1045 BC, divination was not the only Shang preoccupation that led to the writing of texts. The Shang elite and its Zhou successors expended huge wealth and energy in the technology and art of bronze casting, and writing was integral to the creation of these most potent symbols of power and worship.

4
Developments during the Bronze Age

Early Bronze Inscriptions

The earliest inscriptions on bronze date from the late Shang period (*c.* 1200–1045 BC), which also witnessed the production of oracle bones. Discovered at Anyang in Henan province and at sites in the central Yangzi region, Shang bronze objects belonged to members of the royal family and the political elite. Under Zhou rule (1045–221 BC) this social level of ownership continued and even widened. In existence today are probably over ten thousand inscribed vessels, weapons, bells and other bronze objects made before the Qin unification of 221 BC.

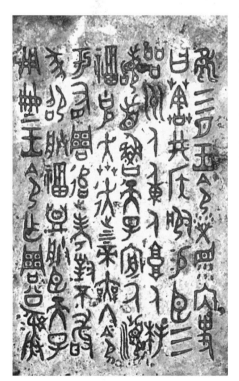

The function of bronze inscriptions
Inscriptions on most weapons are prominent and easily visible. By contrast, inscriptions on vessels of the Shang and the following Western Zhou period (1045–770 BC) were usually placed on the vessels' interior surfaces, where they are much less clearly seen. The inscription photographed for the cover of this book is located on the floor of the Xing Hou *gui* (fig. 4.1), a type of tureen, and will be examined in more detail later.

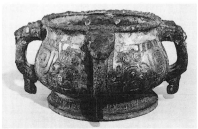

Fig. 4.1 Xing Hou *gui*, late 11th century, H. 18.5 cm, BM (OA) 1936.11-18.2.

33

Sacrificial feasts using inscribed vessels were held to honour and appease ancestral spirits. Most Shang vessel inscriptions state the name of the descent group who commissioned the vessel and identify the ancestor to whom it was dedicated, for instance on this vessel: 'Grandfather Gui of the Ge' *Ge zu Gui* (fig. 4.2).

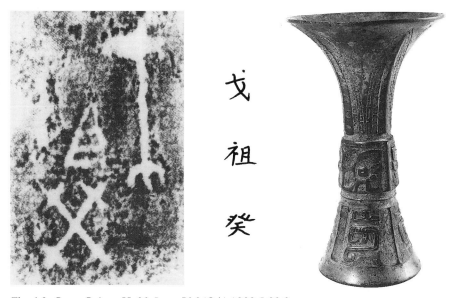

Fig. 4.2 Ge zu Gui *gu*, H. 20.5 cm, BM (OA) 1939.5-22.2.

Ge, also the word for a pole-mounted axe (or dagger), is the group name. That is, the vessel was dedicated by a descendant of the Ge to an ancestor whose sacrifices were due every *gui* (tenth) day, hence his appellation Gui. (This word is to be distinguished from *gui* 'vessel'.) *Zu* 'grandfather' and *fu* 'father' are generic terms that occur in many inscriptions of this period. The brevity of these examples is typical of Shang vessel inscriptions, none of which exceeds forty characters.

Inscriptions on Western Zhou vessels tend to be longer. The vessels were often commissioned in response to appointments and gifts with which the Zhou kings rewarded meritorious service. The inscriptions served as reports intended for a newly honoured individual's ancestors, to whom many early Zhou vessels were dedicated. It was as spiritual communications that inscriptions were placed inside vessels where they were seldom visible. Although the inscriptions were hidden by whatever was put into the vessels during feasts, they were in physical contact with the essential media of food and drink. Inscribed vessels functioned within an atmosphere of fire, cooking smells, music and ritual gestures. The aim on these occasions was quite literally to sate a spirit with food and alcohol. The living participants believed that ancestral spirits embodied in impersonators –

entranced performers especially adept at mediating between the human and spiritual realms – came to take part in the elaborate proceedings. Contact between the spirits and their living descendants was made possible by shared food and drink that had directly touched the inscribed texts. Spirits, once properly catered for, could assist their living descendants in the avoidance of evil.

Writing in a transitional phase

A number of notably depictional signs in the brief bronze inscriptions of the Shang and the early Western Zhou are not yet identified, particularly those related to proper names. The two horses flanking a title and the name of a family group on an early Western Zhou *ding*, a three- or four-legged type of sacrificial vessel, are still undeciphered (fig. 4.3):

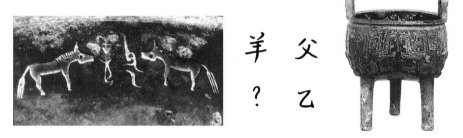

Fig. 4.3 Yang [...?] Fu Yi *ding*, H. 22 cm, BM (OA) 1973.7-26.2.

Between the horses four conventional characters are arranged in two columns that read from left to right. The last two characters give the title Fu Yi 'Father Yi [second day]'. Before this title is the character for 'sheep', used here for the name read Yang. The character below it is not deciphered, but it occurs also in an oracle bone inscription, where it probably represents the name of a social group or a state bordering Shang territory. Thus we read:

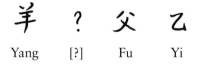

羊	?	父	乙
Yang	[?]	Fu	Yi

'Father Yi of the Yang ...[?]'

The two horses are impossible to interpret satisfactorily. On the basis of an evolutionary theory of writing, in which pictographic signs are seen as a primary phase of any system's invention, these horse depictions might be just such signs that survived the transition from pictographic representation to a system of signs used to represent the sounds of words. The conservative reference to the past that such signs represent is not surprising within the social context of powerful descent groups and their perpetual concern for deceased ancestors. Horses depicted like the ones in this example and other depictions of a similar style seldom feature in oracle bone texts. The oracle bone character for *ma* 'horse' is:

ma 'horse' *c.* 1000 BC   Current form of *ma* 'horse'

Nor do mimetic depictions of horses – like those in the bronze inscription above – and other phenomena seem to have had any role in contemporary texts beyond the context of names. They might have worked like heraldic devices. Their lack of an obvious function analogous to that of characters suggests, however, that such depictions were already dispensable for the future development of Chinese writing.

Technical and artistic developments

Precise practices at different bronze foundries varied, but nearly all inscriptions were prepared on a clay mould and cast from this on to the metal surface of an object. Most inscriptions are countersunk and positive. That is, characters do not rise above the surrounding metal surface, and the text is not a form of mirror-writing (a negative inscription). Inscriptions in relief were occasionally cast, but they became widespread only in association with ironwork in a much later period. Negative inscriptions are extremely rare. Texts were usually arranged in columns reading from right to left.

In order to obtain a positive inscription, the surface of the mould had to be prepared with the text in a negative form. To do this, the text was written with a stylus on a surface of wet clay. When hardened, this positive version could be pressed into a new supply of wet clay to provide a negative relief. Next, the hardened clay of the second version in negative could be trimmed and fitted as a block into an excavation on the mould core of the whole vessel. The mould and this fitting were then ready to receive the molten metal, which would re-form the inscription back into a positive appearance. This method comprises the fewest transfer operations needed to cast a countersunk, positive inscription and allows for the text to be written out freehand in the same form that it will assume in metal.

Bronze inscriptions are thus preservations of calligraphy in the medium of clay. Writing in wet clay offered a wide range of possibilities for variation and liveliness, and even quite early inscriptions show a concern for style. One of the most graceful inscriptions in the British Museum's collection is an extremely short text cast on an early Western Zhou *fang ding* (fig. 4.4), a square, four-legged sacrificial vessel. It is a meticulous casting of the same simple characters for Father Yi (Fu Yi – compare the same inscription in fig. 4.3) below a character for the family group, which has not yet been deciphered.

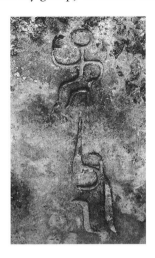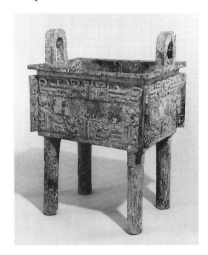

Fig. 4.4 [...?] Fu Yi *fang ding*, H. 24.7 cm, BM (OA) 1947.7-12.422.

The gradual thinning and thickening of line in these characters must have been achieved by drawing a stylus through clay at different angles.

Even in the early Zhou, scribes elaborated considerably. The name Ge, cited in an example above (fig. 4.2), appears on another vessel in the British Museum's collection, an early Western Zhou *ding*. Although we might expect the appearance of Western Zhou writing to have become less complex with the passage of centuries, the inscription on the later *ding* vessel is in fact the more decorative version (fig. 4.5).

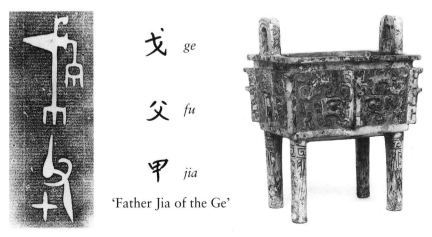

Fig. 4.5 Ge Fu Jia *ding*, H. 27.3 cm, BM (OA) 1973.7-26.3.

These minor increases in complexity reveal a deep conservatism in the development of written forms for bronze inscriptions during the period of Shang and Western Zhou rule. We have no idea whether these habits were paralleled in less formal productions of texts.

The rectangular appearance of bronze-cast texts was clearly important. Forming a text into a rectangle requires forethought in order to distribute the total number of characters into columns so that the last character of the inscription falls precisely in the bottom left-hand corner. The inscription in the Xing Hou *gui* (fig. 4.1), shown on the cover of this book and discussed in detail

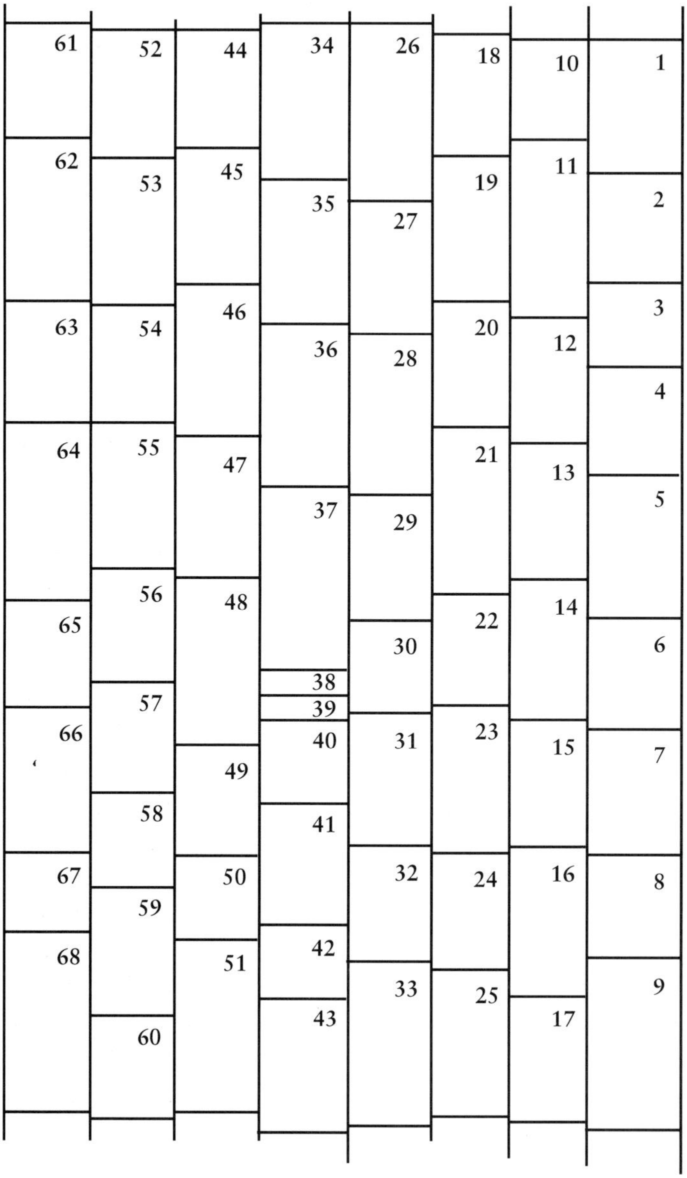

Fig. 4.6 Grid showing the varying heights of characters inscribed in the Xing Hou *gui*.

below, contains 68 characters distributed unevenly among eight columns, read from right to left.

To make their texts fit within a rectangle, Shang and early Zhou inscribers first distributed their texts roughly over whatever number of columns space allowed and then used different heights of characters to cover the discrepancies between the varying numbers of characters in each column. Fig. 4.6 shows a grid taken from the inscription on the Xing Hou *gui*. Its horizontal lines mark the boundaries beneath the lowest extremity of each character. The inscriber of this text arranged the characters in a sequence that fits exactly between the top right and bottom left of a rectangle. Nor did the inscriber allow any element of a single character to stray into the space reserved for the next character below it. The number of characters in a column varies from eight to ten. The differences in character heights was the key to fitting large numbers of characters into limited rectangular spaces. In later centuries, however, when a uniform height for characters had been regularized for many bronze inscriptions, mathematical division must have been essential to planning layouts, and it seems probable that texts were drafted and finalized with a fixed total character count in mind.

Reading Bronze Inscriptions

The sample text discussed here is one of the most famous bronze inscriptions outside China. It appears on a *gui* (fig. 4.1), a food vessel that was probably cast late in the eleventh century BC during the vogue for this form. It is often referred to as 'the *gui* of the Marquis of Xing' (Xing Hou *gui*), who is mentioned in its inscription. Many historians in China and Japan call this vessel the '*gui* for the Duke of Zhou', for this is the illustrious nobleman of the early Zhou to whom the inscription actually dedicates the vessel. It has also been called the Rong *gui*, because the inscription relates that someone called Rong and another unnamed individual actually commissioned it to be made.

The Marquis of Xing was a descendant of the Duke of Zhou, who, according to traditional accounts, helped to establish the Zhou dynasty and ruled as regent during its early existence. Although a somewhat shadowy historical presence, the Duke of Zhou is a major cultural figure to whom legend ascribes the authorship of the Zhou's ritual and musical canons. In the records of Confucius' teachings, known as the *Analects* (*Lunyu*), the sixth-century BC sage mentions the Duke of Zhou repeatedly as the greatest past exemplar of moral and political conduct. Indeed, during the rise of Confucian teaching in subsequent centuries, the Duke of Zhou was co-opted beside Confucius as a leading figure in the Confucian cult.

The following transliteration and a gloss are ordered in eight lines to match the eight columns of the inscription. Numbers refer to the grid in fig. 4.6. Since we can hardly approximate the conditions of early Zhou pronunciation, the transliteration is given in Standard Modern Chinese.

40

COLUMN 1

佳／唯　三　月　王　令／命　焂／榮　眾　內　史

1		2	3	4	5	6	7	8	9
wei		san	yue	wang	ming	Rong	li	nei	shi

Precisely * third * month * king * decreed * Rong * with * inner * scribe

COLUMN 2

曰　籉／句　井／邢　侯　服　易／賜　臣　三

10	11	12	13	14	15	16	17
yue	gai	Xing	Hou	fu	ci	chen	san

announcing * assist * Xing * Marquis * observances * give * servants * three

COLUMN 3

品　州　人　東　董　人　韋／廱　人　拜

18	19	20	21	22	23	24	25
pin	Zhou	ren	Dong	ren	Yong	ren	bai

kinds * Zhou * people * Dong * people * Yong * people * cross hands

COLUMN 4

頤／稽　首　魯　天　子　寁／造　华／厥　瀨／順

26	27	28	29	30	31	32	33
ji	shou	lu	tian	zi	zao	jue	shun

lower * heads * praise * heaven * son * effecting * this * favour

COLUMN 5

福　克　奔　走　上　下　帝　無　冬／終　令／命

34	35	36	37	38	39	40	41	42	43
fu	ke	ben	zou	shang	xia	di	wu	zhong	ming

blessing * able * to reach * to mingle * above * below * Di, the High Ancestor * not * end * mandate

COLUMN 6

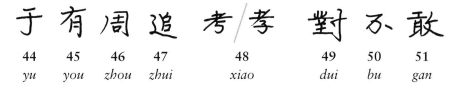

44	45	46	47	48	49	50	51
yu	you	zhou	zhui	xiao	dui	bu	gan

for * existence * Zhou * honour * deceased ancestors * response * not * dare

COLUMN 7

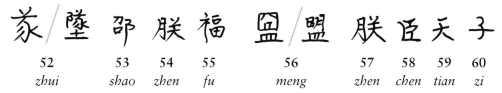

52	53	54	55	56	57	58	59	60
zhui	shao	zhen	fu	meng	zhen	chen	tian	zi

to fail * carry on * our * fortunate * pledge * long * serve * heaven * son

COLUMN 8

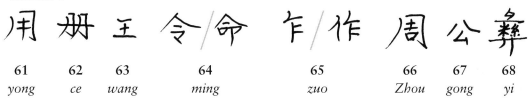

61	62	63	64	65	66	67	68
yong	ce	wang	ming	zuo	Zhou	gong	yi

using * record * king * decree * made * Zhou * Duke * vessel

Translation:

Precisely *in the* third month *the* king *issued his* decree *to* Rong and *the* Inner Court Scribe, announcing: 'Assist *the* Marquis *of* Xing *in his [ritual]* observances! *I* give *you* three kinds *of* servants: Zhou people, Dong people *and* Yong people.' *We [Rong and the Inner Court Scribe]* cross *our* hands *and* lower *our* heads *to* praise *the* son *of* heaven *for* effecting this favour *and* blessing, *which are* able to reach *and* to mingle *[among the spirits]* above *and* below. *May* Di, the High Ancestor, not end *the* mandate *for the* existence *of the* Zhou. *We will* honour *our* deceased ancestors *and in* response *[to this decree] will* not dare to fail *[in our mission]*. *We will* carry on our fortunate pledge *and* long serve *the* son *of* heaven. Using *a* record *of the* king's decree *we* made *this* vessel *for the* Duke *of* Zhou.

This text is a paradigmatic arrangement of common political and religious themes in a standard order. A royal announcement, which orders Rong and the Inner Court Scribe to serve the Marquis of Xing, is followed by a description of the king's gifts to them. Many inscriptions describe gifts of equestrian equipment, weapons and courtly apparel, but this text lists three groups of 'servants', who were probably large numbers of slaves destined for resettlement in the territory of the Marquis of Xing. (The transliteration for one of these groups, Zhou, is identical to that of the Zhou regime, but they are distinct names that imply no particular relationship.) The response by Rong and the Inner Court Scribe contains familiar vessel-inscription themes of gratitude, recognition of the Zhou regime's omnipotence and hope for its eternal survival. This political rhetoric is then modified by a sense of obligation to past ancestors. Articulating ancestral links between living and dead was the fundamental motive for nearly all bronze inscriptions of this period. The text on the Xing Hou *gui* interweaves these links with loyalty to the Zhou and the dedication of the vessel to one of the regime's chief founders.

To decipher what this text says involves identifying its characters, understanding certain processes of phonetic borrowing and recognizing a few patterns of grammar and syntax.

Deciphering characters

One of the most important tools in the process of deciphering this text's characters is a style of writing called seal script, which comprises the epigraphical forms of characters used in the Late Bronze Age and standardized by or shortly before AD 100. More will be said about seal script's history in the following chapter. Its importance for reading very early texts is due to the fact that seal script characters, once they had been prescribed in standard compositions, have continued throughout Chinese history as increasingly archaic forms that can be equated with modern characters as well as with the characters of ancient inscriptions. For example, the following characters can be compared to both seal script and current forms:

Xing Hou *gui*	Seal script	Current forms
三 *san* (2/17)	三	三
夕 *yue* (3)	刀	月
土 *wang* (4/63)	王	王
内 *nei* (8)	内	內
史 *shi* (9)	史	史
天 *tian* (29/59)	天	天
子 *zi* (30/60)	子	子
福 *fu* (34)	福	福
帝 *di* (40)	帝	帝
周 *zhou* (46/66)	周	周

A few characters have likewise retained the basic forms and number of their constituent elements, but undergone transformations of inversion or horizontal switching:

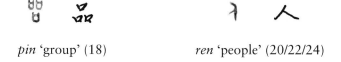

pin 'group' (18)   *ren* 'people' (20/22/24)

Other characters exist in compositions that are no longer current or else bear only a slight resemblance to later forms of these characters. The history of changes to their composition is usually revealing. For example, the character *zao* 'to effect' or 'to cause to be' (31) is composed of a vessel below the roof of a building. Although the 'vessel' element also provided the character's phonetic reading, a sacrificial vessel and a temple building were combined for a word meaning 'effect', since its action involved sacrifices to invoke spiritual powers in temple settings. Some forms of this character contain an extra element on the right whose meaning was 'report', but its primary function, according to later commentators, was as the character's phonetic element:

Many other meanings were associated with this word, including those for the actions of going and arriving, so the character sometimes appears with the addition of a determinative below, which is used for meanings of motion or travel. The following example includes this determinative, but the roof of the building has been eliminated:

By contrast, there exist three bronze vessels with inscriptions that employ a form of the character combining only the 'vessel' with the determinative for motion. Finally, by the end of the Bronze Age, the character was standardized as a semantic and phonetic combination of two elements, which includes neither of the two elements used to write the character on the Xing Hou *gui*:

Late Bronze Age composition of *zao*   Current form of *zao*

This brief survey of developments shows how deciphering ancient characters often requires an accurate sense of how certain characters are ancestral to later forms. The links are important because, once they are understood, a large philological literature dating from the end of the Bronze Age is available to help in interpreting characters that would otherwise remain quite unfamiliar and meaningless. The first compilation to address the use of determinatives systematically and thereby attempt to control multivalent character usage is the *Shuowen jiezi* dictionary. China's first comprehensive etymological dictionary, its title means 'to comment on proper forms and to analyze characters'. Completed in AD 100 by Xu Shen (80–124), this work arranges the material according to five hundred determinatives. Most Chinese dictionaries today use a system of 214 determinatives, which was first proposed at the end of the Ming dynasty (AD 1368–1644). Xu Shen aimed to help scholars of his day read the ancient scripts inherited from the period before China's unification in 221 BC, as familiarity with these scripts was already beginning to decline. This motive for the compilation of the *Shuowen* makes the work a vital bridge linking Chinese writing from the ancient and modern worlds.

Phonetic borrowings

The first character of the Xing Hou *gui* inscription, *wei*, is a grammatical particle that introduces most narrative texts of the Bronze Age, but it possesses no direct English equivalent. The character for this word is a phonetic borrowing of the character for 'bird' (now pronounced *zhui*), and the bird-like form of the character is reflected in the decorative flourishes that the inscriber used on the Xing Hou *gui*. *Wei* usually appears in a more muted style, as shown by two more examples to the right of the Xing Hou *gui* character:

The third example, which appears on another early Western Zhou inscription (the Lu Hou *zun*, a type of drinking vessel, now in the Shanghai Museum), is the character *wei* including a 'mouth' determinative on the left. It is an early instance of a determinative used to distinguish the meaning of *wei* as a grammatical particle.

Other phonetic borrowings include the characters *li* (7), discussed in ch. 2, and *gai* (11), meaning respectively 'with' and 'assist'. Modern interpretations of the character *gai* differ. It is thought to be a phonetic borrowing either for a word meaning 'to give' or for an alternative 'to assist'. Both meanings fit well in the present text.

The character *zhen* (54/57) illustrates the multivalent use of a character for more than one word. It is used once for the first person pronoun 'I' or 'we' – texts seldom distinguish which – but it appears in a second instance for a semantically distinct but homophonous word 'long'. Exactly which word it stands for is difficult to identify, but other texts containing the stock phrase 'may I ever serve ...' contain one or other of two characters now read *jun* and *nong* occurring where the Xing Hou *gui* inscription uses *zhen*. The character for the word now read as *nong* can be understood as 'loyal', and that meaning has been adopted in this translation. Although this reading is tentative, comparison with other texts shows at least that a character located before the verb *chen* 'to serve' is a modifying adverb.

A few rules of syntax and grammar

Vessel inscriptions nearly always begin with a monthly date or an event, which Zhou readers apparently understood as a reference to a particular moment in their recent history: 'It was when the king was in such-and-such a place'. All these formulae are introduced with the particle *wei* (1), discussed above. The date is usually given as a month, shown by a number and the character *yue* (3), which stands for both 'moon' and 'month'.

Direct speech is introduced with the verb *yue* (10) 'announced'. There is no indication of where a speech closes other than the resumption of the narrative, which occurs at *ci* (15). If they are included, other verbs of speech and their objects precede *yue*. In fact, the text states that the king 'decreed' certain people before recording his announcement.

Certain combinations observe a rule that dependent elements follow whatever they are subordinate to, for example:

Xing Hou (12–13)	'Marquis *of* Xing'
Zhou ren (19–20)	'people *from* Zhou' (i.e. 'Zhou people')
tian zi (29–30)	'son *of* heaven'
Zhou gong yi (66–8)	'vessel *of the* Duke of Zhou'

Numbers and other attributes follow what they modify. Thus, the king's gift is stated as: 'servants – three kinds', as opposed to the familiar English order in the translation: 'three kinds *of* servants'.

Characters often represented words in more than one grammatical role. Even though modern grammar is different, this versatility is still a feature of the modern language (see ch. 2). *Chen* (16/58) 'servant' acts in its first occurrence in the Xing Hou *gui* inscription as a noun, but in its second as a verb, 'to serve'. Also performing more than one grammatical role is the character standing for both the verb 'to decree' *ming* (5) and the semantically related nouns 'decree' and 'mandate' *ming* (43/64).

This effective use of the same characters in different grammatical roles considerably reduces a text's number of characters. Indeed, the Xing Hou *gui* inscription is 68 characters long, but uses only 57 different characters.

The development of writing in the Western Zhou

The number of characters in this text that subsequently dropped out of common use is as few as two (7 and 11). The rest, undergoing different degrees of change, have circulated until today. The inscription on the Xing Hou *gui* includes characters that were ultimately modified by the addition of particular determinatives. Although the number of these characters is slight, they are an important indication of the developments of early writing. The text's first character, *wei*, discussed above, is a prime example. Likewise, the marquis' name Xing (12) uses a character that would ultimately assume a new and distinct form. The character on the Xing Hou *gui* was used also for *jing* 'water well'. Naturally, context helps to decide which meaning is intended, but later texts distinguished the two words by adding a determinative, used for words denoting any kind of human settlement, to the name Xing. This is how it appears within the rectangular border of a bronze seal *c.* 200 BC, which is illustrated again in fig. 5.5:

The history of the character *zhong* (42) shows a similar development. Its meaning 'to end' was extended to another meaning, *dong* 'winter', the season that *ends* a year. Both words were written with the character shown in the Xing Hou *gui*. This character and its later form show ends of hanging silk:

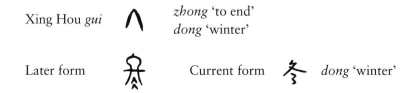

Xing Hou *gui*   *zhong* 'to end'
                   dong 'winter'

Later form   Current form   *dong* 'winter'

Later writers, however, distinguished the verb 'to end' by adding a determinative, itself also a depiction of silk, shown as an element on the left of a new character:

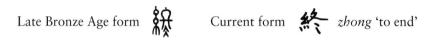

Late Bronze Age form   Current form   *zhong* 'to end'

In the early history of Chinese writing, determinatives were gradual accretions to a system in which multivalence was the dominant feature. The most difficult problems of interpretation today frequently arise from these instances of multivalence, and it is evident that scholars in the Late Bronze Age also perceived that a greater degree of control was needed.

The inscription on the Xing Hou *gui* is an early text, and the developmental status of some of its characters is correspondingly primitive. Remarkably, however, it is still possible to decipher and interpret meanings for nearly all of these characters. Some of these can be applied in reading hundreds more bronze inscriptions, but the most forceful expressions of the early Zhou political and religious outlook were gradually eroded: invocations to the 'Son of Heaven' (*tianzi*) became almost eccentric and dedications to specific ancestors became much rarer. Even so, in north China during the following centuries, the early Zhou legacy of its script endured in a substantially more conservative form compared to more adventurous developments in the south, which are considered next.

Late Bronze Age Ornate Scripts in South China

In 770 BC, no longer able to withstand invasions from further west, the Zhou government in north-west China collapsed. The regime relocated eastwards to Luoyang, but its authority over surrounding areas was drastically diminished. During this period, which is known as the Eastern Zhou (770–221 BC), what we now know as China was effectively divided into a number of regional states which aimed to survive through strategic combinations of war and alliance. Linguistic developments were far from even within several zones of government covering vast regions. Moreover, striking innovations in style and form characterize the inscriptions of this period, since within a decentralized political landscape writing developed at multiple centres of court patronage.

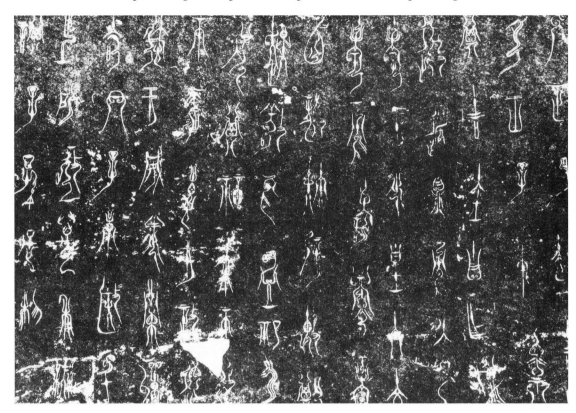

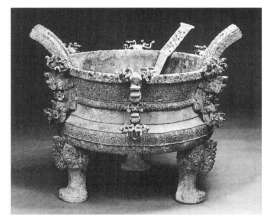

Fig. 4.7 Inscription in a *shengding* of the Chu state, mid-6th century BC, H. of inscribed surface approx. 30 cm, excav. Henan province 1978. After *Wenwu*, 1980.10: pl.12; and *shengding*, one of seven vessels, inscribed with the same inscription. After Henan Sheng Wenwu Yanjiusuo, *Xichuan Xiasi chunqiu Chu mu*, Beijing, 1991: fig. 101.

South China saw the development of new script forms unparalleled in the north. The dominant cultural focus of south China was the state of Chu, whose large territory extended from the central Yangzi region to a frontier zone not far south of the traditional seats of Zhou rule, near the modern cities of Xi'an and Luoyang. The inscription in fig. 4.7 is one of seven almost identical versions placed inside the same number of tripod *ding* vessels.

Although this is not apparent in a rubbing, the inscription's fourteen columns flow down the vessel's wall and then, near the base, turn ninety degrees to continue on the horizontal surface of the vessel floor. This tall and trailing script was developed in several variations, and today it is often termed *kedouwen*, 'tadpole script'.

The text on this vessel relates that Prince Wu (d. 552 BC) commissioned it in honour of his grandfather, the Chu king Wen Wang (r. 689–676 BC), and then lengthily extols Prince Wu's own virtuous qualities. Although most inhabitants of Chu spoke a different language to the population of north China, the syntactical variations between written language in north and south were minor. All inscriptions of this period, however, display considerable differences in the composition of particular characters, notably in the use of determinatives. In Prince Wu's text (fig. 4.7), for example, in the standard concluding expression *wan nian wu qi*, 'ten thousand years without limit', the inscriber uses an unusual form of character for the final word:

The same combination of elements stands today for the word *qi* 'to deceive'. That is not the meaning intended here. On the right is the phonetic element, which, if isolated, is the character for 'basket', now pronounced *qi*, and to the left is the 'speech' determinative. The same phonetic appears also in the common Late Bronze Age form of *qi* 'limit', which incorporates the 'sun' determinative at the character's base:

The positioning of determinatives within a character was still quite fluid. A northern bronze vessel from the same period, a *ding* made in the minor state of Su (located around modern Wenxian in Henan province), provides a variant in the form of a small circle at the top of the character:

A later combination shows the 'moon' determinative beside the same *qi* phonetic, the form in which the character is composed today:

No matter which determinative is present, all four combinations above share a common phonetic element. Writing the character with the 'speech' determinative, however, raises the most glaring ambiguity. But, although the modern reading of *qi* 'to deceive' is totally inappropriate in this instance, it poses only a minor problem of interpretation, since the context of a standard expression dictates the reader's understanding of *qi* 'limit'. What comparisons of these characters show is that the phonetic values of characters were often more important than the specific meanings which attached determinatives offered. This led to a great deal of phonetic borrowing, particularly in texts from Chu and other southern states.

Southern bronze inscriptions also differ from northern productions in the radical ornamentation of their calligraphy. Chu inscriptions developed elongated characters composed of highly involved patterns of almost razor-thin swirls.

This sophisticated writing style was perfectly suited to inscriptions displayed prominently on the exterior surfaces of vessels, bells, weapons and other objects. In the lower Yangzi valley states of Wu and Yue, from the sixth century BC onwards, inscriptions on bronze weaponry were placed on the blade and inlaid in gold or turquoise. A particularly lavish expression of these practices used a script called 'bird script' (*niaoshu*), which incorporated feather-like flows in its schematic profiles of birds. Like inscriptions on contemporary vessels, these texts on weapons concentrate on the individuals who commissioned them.

Bird script decorates King Zhu Gou's gold-inlaid spearhead in the British Museum (fig. 4.8).

Fig. 4.8 Bronze spearhead inlaid with gold and inscribed in bird script, H. 28.6 cm, BM (OA) 1947.7-12.426.

Zhu Gou (r. 448–412 BC) ruled the state of Yue in the lower Yangzi valley. Several Yue rulers' names appear on deluxe weapons produced from the early fifth century BC onwards, but Zhu Gou's occurs most frequently. The script on these weapons, which was a cultural hallmark of Yue, demanded extremely delicate casting. A Yue sword in the Shanghai Museum bears the four characters of a royal name in the wrong sequence. This suggests that some system of inserting individual characters into a mould was used, and the awkward result on the Shanghai sword proves that the practice went awry at least once.

Reading the two columns from right to left, the eight characters of the inscription on the British Museum's spearhead state:

越	王	州	句	自	乍/作	用	矛
Yue	*wang*	*Zhou* for *Zhu Gou*		*zi*	*zuo*	*yong*	*mao*
'[The] Yue	king	Zhu	Gou'	'himself [had]	made	[for his own] use	[this] spear'

Comparison of these characters with those on the Xing Hou *gui* (fig. 4.1) shows that, except for their added swirls and bird forms, they are essentially similar. The second column of the following table shows four characters from the sword inscription divested of their bird-like embellishments and compared to the same characters used in the Xing Hou *gui* inscription:

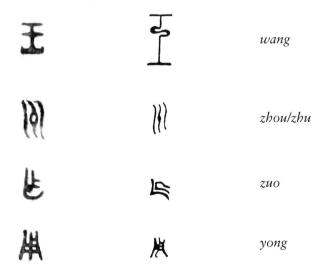

		wang
		zhou/zhu
		zuo
		yong

In its full form, bird script was difficult to write, and the skills required were clearly not widespread. Indeed, some bird-script inscriptions contain characters that are stiffly adjusted to the fluent decoration attached to them. A few characters appear without any decorative integration at all. Significantly, since most of these inscriptions consist of eight characters or fewer, the use of a restricted number of characters avoided the need for an intensive redevelopment of a large number of characters in new and complex forms.

Tension between decorative design and legibility exists in most ornate scripts, but the ornateness of the bird script of south-east China is extreme. Texts in this script were so elaborate that they became almost illegible. In fact, the inscriptions on Yue weapons acquired by collectors in the late nineteenth century were not deciphered for several decades. Their decorative style and textual arrangements virtually abandoned any demand for legibility. The characters for Zhu Gou's name are repeated symmetrically to fill both halves of a guard on a sword now in Paris (fig. 4.9). This double inscription served more to decorate the guard evenly than to offer a legible statement.

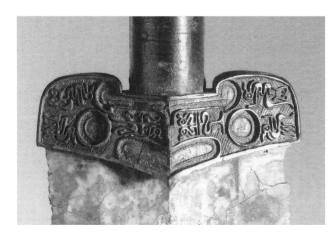

Fig. 4.9 Inscription on a sword guard, late 5th century BC, D. 4.1 cm, Musée Cernuschi, Paris, MC 08621. ©Phototheque de Musées de la Ville de Paris.

Although stylistic developments of script in north China were generally less radical, the appearance of inscriptions there was sometimes influenced by southern ornateness. An outstanding example is the square *hu* vase, datable to 309 or 308 BC, which was excavated in 1977 from the royal cemetery of the Zhongshan kingdom near Pingshan in central Hebei province. The inscriber, whose role was clearly the most significant of all the artists involved in this complicated production, has covered the four sides of the vessel with a long text of 450 characters describing the Zhongshan state's most recent territorial expansion (fig. 4.10).

This text is considerably easier to read than the highly embellished characters found on slightly earlier bronze objects from south-east China. In fact, its greater legibility places it much closer to the developments in script styles that took place in the north and had the greatest influence on Chinese writing during and after the unification of China in the third century BC.

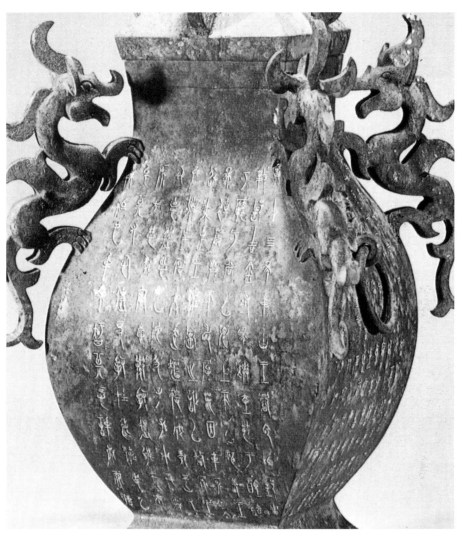

Fig. 4.10 Bronze *hu* vessel from tomb of King Cuo of the Zhongshan kingdom, H. 62 cm, 4th century BC, excav. Hebei province 1977. After *Cuo mu: zhanguo Zhongshan guo guowang zhi mu*, Beijing, 1995: pl. 7.

5
Writing in a
Unified Empire

New Standards and Scripts

Towards the end of the Warring States period (475–221 BC) the western kingdom of Qin became the strongest state of all. It eliminated its enemies and unified their territories to create the first Chinese empire under the Qin dynasty. Although the Qin empire lasted less than two decades (221–207 BC), its impact on the development of writing is difficult to exaggerate. The script reforms instituted by the Qin government did not represent sudden decisions: they reflected developments that had matured over several centuries within the borders of Qin's traditional territory.

The standards established during the Qin period represent a milestone in the history of writing. Prior to China's unification, writing in Qin and other states differed stylistically (sometimes radically so, in the case of the south-eastern states and Chu) but all used the same writing system. Even so, the ubiquitous process of phonetic borrowing produced different ways of writing the same word in different regions of China. For instance, *chu* 'kitchen', updated to current forms, could be written with changing combinations of determinatives and phonetics:

朕	庶	胆	廚	厨
Northern states		Chu (south)	Qin (west)	Current composition

These highly distinct characters, used to write the same word, were not scribal errors. On the eve of Qin unification this phenomenon, which later ages would regard as a state of chaos, had become more widespread than ever before.

The Qin state had witnessed the development of a formal and balanced writing style which is usually called seal script. Surviving Qin inscriptions show the appearance of writing in two broad contexts: formal pronouncements and commemorations, which used seal script; and administrative records and other texts not used for commemorative purposes, which adopted the workaday 'clerical script' (*lishu*), a script already well developed by the time of China's imperial unification. This formal and functional duality is also noticeable in Chu inscriptions and in those of other states of the late Warring States period, but the Qin forms are particularly well documented, and they achieved the most lasting effect throughout China as a whole. Measures undertaken by the Qin government also established a firm basis for the later development of several major forms of brush writing: the cursive scripts (*caoshu* and *xingshu*) and 'regular' or 'model' script (*kaishu*), which represents the last major development for Chinese script as it appears today.

Seal script

Seal script (*zhuanwen*) is the script that Xu Shen adopted as a standard for the entries in his *Shuowen jiezi*, and, as previous chapters have shown, it remains one of the major bridges for deciphering even the earliest inscriptions. The term *zhuan* means to carve or work a plastic material, and *zhuanwen* was largely reserved for carving and casting inscriptions. Following the formation of the Qin empire, it became the leading script used for personal and official seals, and it is this association that gave rise to its name. But inscriptions on other objects also employed seal script. One of these is the Qin Gong *gui* (fig. 5.1), cast in the late

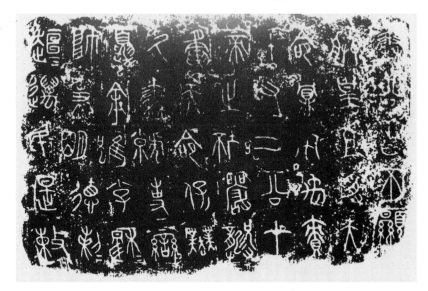

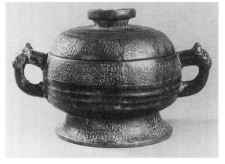

Fig. 5.1 Part of the Qin Gong *gui* inscription in the vessel body. After Gao Ming, *Zhongguo guwenzixue tonglun*, Beijing, 1987: fig. 101; and Qin Gong *gui*, H. 19.8 cm, excav. Gansu province 1923, Chinese History Museum, Beijing. After *Chūgoku rekishi hakubutsukan*, Beijing/Kyoto, 1982: no. 60.

sixth century BC, which bears an inscription showing an early appearance of seal script. Remarkably, each character in this inscription was formed by an individual seal pressed into the damp clay of the vessel's mould core.

Dedicated to the Duke of Qin, head of state in the period before the Qin adopted royal titles, the script on this vessel clearly represents a formal chancellery script used in the same way as bird script in the south-eastern state of Yue. The following chart shows six characters from the Qin Gong *gui* compared both to seal script forms and to characters inscribed on the Xing Hou *gui*:

Xing Hou *gui*	Qin Gong *gui*	Seal script	Current forms	
				yue 'to announce'
				Di (name)
				bu 'not'
				zhen 'I'
				tian 'heaven'
				gong 'duke'

The basic conservatism of Qin script was that, over a longer period that any other state, it so closely followed forms inherited from the Western Zhou. Qin was located in the north-west, and its borders enclosed former Western Zhou territory. However, as the table shows, Qin scribes aimed for a greater degree of balance. The characteristic formal script of the Qin empire, represented here by the seal script examples in the third column, was already considerably developed as early as the sixth century BC. Qin seal script of some three hundred years later was rendered more fluently, but the balance and composition of individual characters underwent few if any dramatic changes. In fact, changes in Qin writing style were much slower than in other states of the Warring States period, many of which were culturally far advanced of Qin even until the eve of the imperial unification.

Seal script has been enormously influential in China's rich history of seal-cutting. Seals appear in the archaeological record from the fifth century BC onwards. Official seals were square. They were cast in metal or carved from stone, wood and bone, and their inscriptions were cut in reverse. One of the primary functions of a seal was to authenticate official documents with their author's name or official title by pressing an inscription into the clay that secured the document's bindings (fig. 5.6 below). Usually the clay was placed in a wooden holder that was slotted to hold the binding cords (fig. 5.2). Later, exactly the same seals were first dipped into red paste and then stamped on to flat surfaces, such as wood or paper.

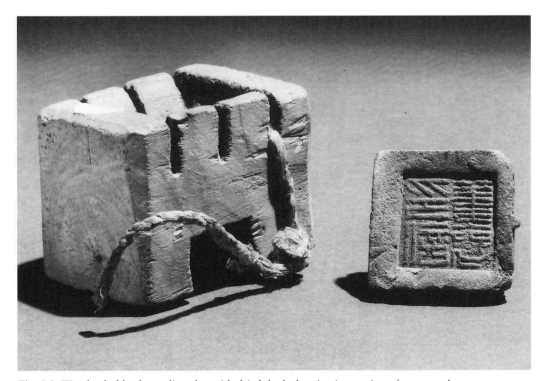

Fig. 5.2 Wooden holder for sealing clay with dried daub showing impression of a personal seal for a man surnamed Dong, Western Han dynasty (206 BC–AD 8), H. 3.6 cm, excav. Gansu province, early 20th century. BM (MAS) 765 and 786.

In a campaign whose significance was as much symbolic as practical, seal script was used to disseminate the edict of 221 BC – one of the empire's founding texts – lauding the new government's efforts to unify weights and measures. These texts of forty characters feature on a number of bronze and ceramic measuring vessels. Significantly, the same text appears on several ceramic vessels as a series of ten seal impressions, each stamped impression bearing four characters of the text. Seal script may have been slow to write, but the swift process of stamping ten units of four characters into wet clay was a triumph of bureaucratic economy and speed (fig. 5.3).

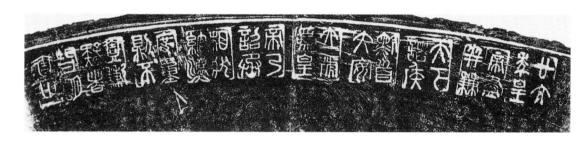

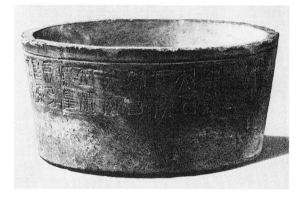

Fig. 5.3 Ceramic measuring vessel, excav. Shandong province 1963, Shandong Provincial Museum. After Zhongguo Lishi Bowuguan et al., eds, *Zhongguo gudai duliangheng tuji*, Beijing, 1984: no. 112.

The Qin and several subsequent dynasties also employed seal script for naming coin issues (fig. 5.4).

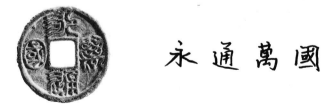

Fig. 5.4 Silver issue of a Northern Zhou coin inscribed *yong tong wan guo* 'Eternally circulated through all kingdoms', first issued in bronze AD 579, D. 3.0 cm, BM (CM) 1996-2-17-250.

Seals and other objects inscribed in seal script show the high degree of standardization achieved by the Qin government. During this period there was growing recognition of the need to dispel the ambiguities that arose from using one character for two or more meanings. For instance, a seal belonging to an individual bearing the same name as the Marquis of Xing shows the character for Xing with a determinative on the right in order to distinguish it from the character for the word for 'water well' (now read *jing*). Commonly, seal script forms of this character show the centre of the 'well' containing an additional dot or, as in this case, a crossing bar (fig. 5.5).

Fig. 5.5 Seal inscribed with family name Xing, H. of seal approx. 1.0 cm, Hunan Province Museum. After Tong Chenyi, ed., *Hunan sheng bowuguan cang gu xiyin ji*, Shanghai, 1991: 19.

To a higher degree than ever before, the characters' determinatives assumed standard forms and were written in fixed positions. Variant phonetic components used in different regions were gradually eliminated.

Clerical script

Seal script is not suitable for composing long documents or for writing at speed. The faster, workaday script of the Qin and Han empires was called *lishu,* 'clerical script', and it was essentially a way of writing seal script without devoting too much time and effort to balanced curves and symmetry. It was also heavily influenced by the use of brush and ink.

Over the past century some spectacular finds of texts written on wooden strips and boards have turned up in archaeological excavations. A small number of writings on silk and some fragments of inscribed paper have also appeared.

Long texts were written on wooden or bamboo strips, and this is how literary writings would almost invariably have appeared to the teacher and philosopher Kong Zi (Confucius, *c.* 551–479 BC). Although archaeological discoveries of strips do not predate the Warring States period (475–221 BC), convincing statements from transmitted writings tell us that wooden strips were used earlier. Besides, we can fairly imagine that the long texts inscribed on bronzes of earlier periods must have had counterparts in cheaper and less unwieldy media. Apart from transmitting histories and canonical scriptures, wooden strips were used to record tracts about medicine, divination and military strategy.

Writing on strips was ordered from left to right and top to bottom. The strips were bound with two lengths of flax or silk cord, either before or after the text was written on them (fig. 5.6).

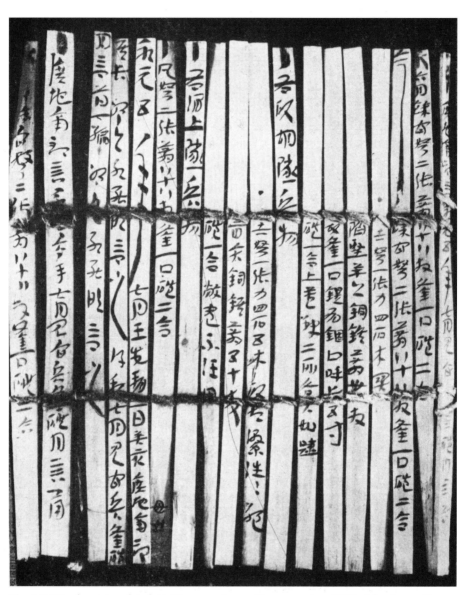

Fig. 5.6 Wooden strips, dated AD 93, excav. Juyan, Gansu province 1973. After *Juyan Han jian jia bian*, Beijing, 1959: pl. 3.

The entire series could be rolled up and tied with the ends of the binding cords. In order to mark a document's ownership or to keep it confidential, the knot was packed with a dab of wet clay and then impressed with a seal. The surface of the bamboo or wood was pared and smoothed with a sharp blade, by which mistakes could be erased or even whole strips cleaned for reuse (fig. 5.7).

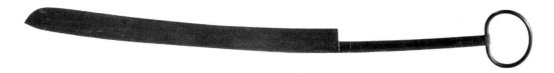

Fig. 5.7 Bronze blade, L. 27 cm, excav. Hubei province 1965. Hubei Provincial Museum, Wuhan. Photo China Cultural Relics Promotion Centre, Beijing.

Excavated tombs and art of the Han period (206 BC–AD 220) suggest that blades rather than brushes were the most emblematic possessions of a Han scholar's status. Loop-handled blades appear hanging from the belts of officials depicted in Han murals, and at funerals such blades were placed with valuable swords inside the deceased's coffin.

Ink was made from a basic recipe of carbon and resin. During this period and later, many and varied forms of inkstone were produced. The example in fig. 5.8 features a pool surrounded by mountains – the legendary habitat for immortals and gods – which symbolizes writing as a divine pursuit.

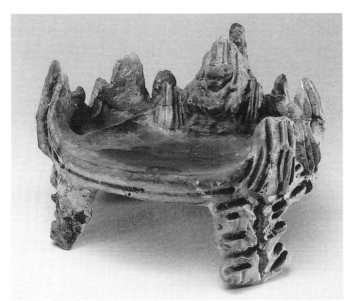

Fig. 5.8 Ceramic inkstone, Eastern Han dynasty (AD 25–220), H. 10 cm, Musée Cernuschi, Paris, MC 09425. ©Phototheque de Musées de la Ville de Paris.

A spectacular find in 1975 was a Qin tomb containing over 1150 bamboo strips. Situated at Shuihudi in the marshy land around the town of Yunmeng, some 90 km north-west of Wuhan, the tomb belonged to a man named Teng (*c.* 262–217 BC), a local official in the Qin 'Southern Command' (Nanjun), which controlled a large territory on the north bank of the central Yangzi river. The texts on the bamboo strips, which were placed around his body in the coffin, largely concerned questions of law and divination. They provide a particularly rich source of writing in Qin clerical script (*lishu*).

The following table shows several characters from the Shuihudi bamboo strips compared with seal script and current forms of characters already encountered in this book:

Clerical script	Seal script	Current forms	
天	而	天	*tian* 'heaven'
仌	訚	公	*gong* 'duke'
与	弓	父	*fu* 'father'
叓	叓	史	*shi* 'scribe'
斆	斆	學	*xue* 'school'
用	用	用	*yong* 'to use'

As these examples show, a priority of clerical script was to retain the separable elements of seal script characters in a sparer form: the number of strokes was lessened; double or triple curves were contracted to single curves or lines; certain minor elements were eliminated. The difference is further illustrated by two jade seals discovered in a Qin tomb. Both were cut with the same two characters for the name Ling Xian, one in seal script and the other in clerical script (fig. 5.9).

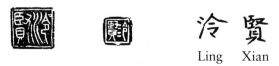

冷　賢
Ling　Xian

Fig. 5.9 Impressions from two jade seals inscribed with the name Ling Xian, Qin dynasty (221–207 BC), excav. Hubei province 1975. After *Wenwu* 1978.2: 50.

There are fewer strokes on the second seal, and the lines of the 'water' determinative in the right half of the seal, for instance, have been reduced to three dots. Most of the curves have been eliminated from both characters. The use of clerical script on seals is unusual, so this example provides an interesting measure of the acceptance that clerical script had gained as a writing style in Qin society.

Early historical sources attribute the invention of clerical script to a Qin official named Cheng Mao (fl. 221 BC), who during a ten-year prison sentence created a lexicon of three thousand characters in a new style of script. It is difficult to accept that one individual performed in ten years what archaeological evidence shows took place over decades or even longer. What this account probably reflects is that Cheng Mao could have assumed a genuine role in first codifying a set of standards for a script that had already begun to develop well before his own lifetime. Certainly, for the Qin government, the standardization of writing was an urgent policy, and the Qin was a defining period for the coherence and unity of Chinese writing that still exists today.

Clerical script remained the commonest script during the Han dynasty (206 BC– AD 220) and it is the style most usually seen as representative of that period. It continued in widespread usage throughout the centuries leading up to the foundation of the Tang dynasty (AD 618–907), and it was often adopted for the finest stone inscriptions of the period. The use of this script certainly declined after the beginning of the seventh century, but a succession of major calligraphers ensured its survival as an enduring strand within China's artistic tradition.

Archaism

The scripts codified under the short-lived Qin government remained influential throughout Chinese history, but during the Han period there was also an evident interest in archaic forms that were disappearing gradually from common use.

Xu Shen's dictionary also included several hundred characters of 'ancient script' (guwen). Xu Shen believed – or claimed to believe – that these forms were the ancient forerunners of seal script. In fact, their forms probably originated during the late Warring States period among the southern and eastern states at the same time as Qin seal script was maturing in the west. But views of so-called ancient script were bound up with arguments about the authority of certain ancient texts and only intensified the political character of the argument about the script's antiquity. A long-running controversy continued even after the fall of the Han dynasty in AD 220, and one of its most lasting products was the carving of several canonical scriptures on stone using three styles of writing: ancient script, seal script and clerical script (fig. 5.10).

The hierarchy of these three scripts, one above the other with ancient script on top, would have reflected cultural priorities, even though it is highly questionable whether scholars still read ancient script with the same degree of fluency as the

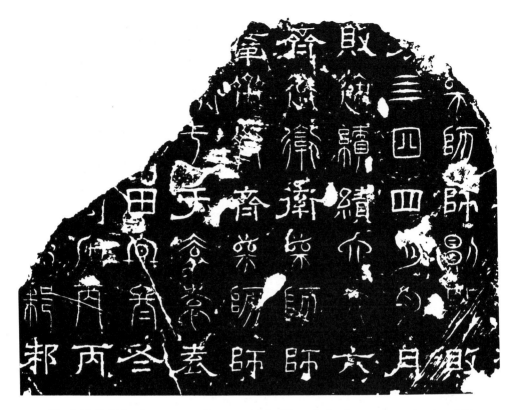

Fig. 5.10 Rubbing from a stone fragment of the 'Three Scripts' canon, completed AD 241, showing each character written in three different scripts, H. 38.3 cm. The second column from the right shows forms of the characters *si* 'four' and *yue* 'month'. After Shaanxi Province History Museum, *Xi'an beilin shufa yishu*, Xi'an, 1983, rev. ed., 1997: 45.

other two. Still, archaistic references like this exerted an enormous pull on the scholarly imagination and symbolized a strong sense of political legitimacy for successive governments. The 'Three Scripts' canons, first placed in the university precincts at Luoyang during the Wei dynasty (AD 220–65), were later removed to the capital of the Northern Qi (550–77), located slightly north of Anyang. In 579 the Northern Zhou government (557–81) returned them to Luoyang. In 586, following the Sui reunification of China, they were brought to the new capital of Chang'an (modern Xi'an). Invading Tang armies smashed them, and the fragments were seldom viewed again until the twentieth century. Scholarly interest in this particular form of ancient script never recovered from this violence. It was only in the twentieth century that archaeological discoveries of Chu writings on silk proved conclusively that the script was a modification of the decorative tadpole scripts beloved of Chu inscribers and their imitators during the late Warring States period.

Seal script survived into the modern period, but early on it became steadily more restricted to specific contexts. Most coins minted between the Qin and the Five Dynasties (AD 907–60) used seal script, but from the tenth century onwards other writing styles began to appear on new issues of coins (see below) and later paper currency. Seal script also enjoyed a vogue as the decorative script for the titles of stone monuments and gravestones between the sixth and tenth centuries, particularly during the Tang dynasty (AD 618–907) (fig. 5.11). Finally, although many forms of script have been adapted for seals, seal script has remained in use and has enjoyed almost continual government sanction as the formal script for inscribing official seals.

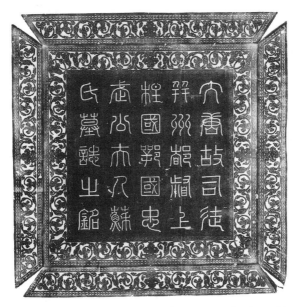

Fig. 5.11 Rubbing from the stone epitaph cover made in AD 659 for the noblewoman Su Wu (589–613), L. of edge 99 cm, stone located Zhaoling Museum, Liquan county, Shaanxi province, rubbing coll. BM (OA) 1997.2-7.124.

Cursive and regular scripts

The standardization of writing and its growing recognition as an art saw their longest period of development during the Han (206 BC–AD 220). The close of the Han and the following period witnessed the rise of cursive scripts, most notably *caoshu* and *xingshu*, and 'regular script' (*kaishu*). *Cao* stands for the meaning 'rough' or 'unfinished', and the combination *caoshu* is therefore rendered as 'draft script'. The word *xing* means 'to move' or 'to run', and it describes a 'running script', with more fluent forms than either clerical or seal script. *Xingshu* later developed fluency to the extent of not lifting the brush between characters. *Kai* is a word for 'model', but the commonest translation of *kaishu* is 'regular script'.

Many commentaries have been written about the development of these scripts, which have provided staple forms in the art of calligraphy from the late Han onwards. None of these scripts developed independently, as there were long periods of chronological overlap and mutual borrowing during their formation. Draft script abbreviates characters so that they can be written faster, a process apparent as early as the Qin period. Bamboo strips from the tomb of officer Teng at Shuihudi show characters in clerical script that already approach the fluency and form characteristic of draft script, model script and even current forms of Chinese writing:

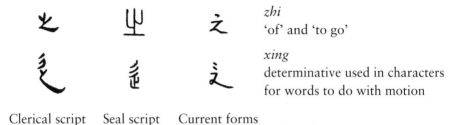

zhi
'of' and 'to go'

xing
determinative used in characters for words to do with motion

Clerical script   Seal script   Current forms

Running script developed similarly, but scholars generally consider it a distinct writing style that arose at the end of the Han period. The most important feature of both these cursive scripts is the reduction of the parts or even the whole of a character to swiftly directed lines. Dating to a much later period, the following three examples of the character *ze* 'pond', produced by three of the most famous medieval exponents of cursive writing, reveal varying degrees of fluency that were all possible in each of their three lifetimes: in Mi Fei's writing all elements of the character are separately discernible; Yan Zhenqing characteristically rendered the three dots of the 'water' determinative as a swaying line. Emperor Taizong formed a heavy dot at the top left and then wrote the rest of the character in a single stroke (fig. 5.12).

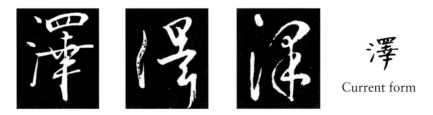

Current form

Fig. 5.12 The character *ze* 'pond' written by Mi Fei (1051–1107), Yan Zhenqing (709–84) and Taizong (r. 626–49). After entries in Wang Baoming, ed., *Zhongguo xingcao shufa dazidian*, Beijing, 1992.

The development of cursive styles in fig. 5.12 also owed much to the establishment of regular script, since the latter provided a basis of orthodoxy against which cursive writers could exercise their own more personal innovations.

Regular script, however, can also be said to have arisen from cursive writing. It can be described as a formalized form of running script, that is to say a cursive script rendered less spare and fluent. The distinctive feature of regular script is that the component elements of characters are all clearly distinguishable, their number and complexity having been largely defined within the developments of clerical script. Thus particular details, determinatives for instance, are delineated more precisely than in the swift cursive convention. The earliest known exponent of regular script was Zhong You (AD 151–230), who just survived the Han dynasty (fig. 5.13).

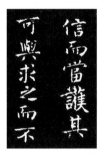

Fig. 5.13 Detail from a rubbing of a memorial by Zhong You (AD 151–230), cut on stone in 1109, possibly following a copy of Zhong You's text made by Wang Xizhi (307–65), Palace Museum, Beijing. After Qi Gong and Wang Jingxian, eds, *Zhongguo meishu quanji*, 'Shufa', vol. 2, Beijing, 1986: no. 12.

Zhong You's biographers record that his model script was a form of running script used in official documents that could be read by a wider than usual readership. It was precisely this tension between the degree of legibility needed in official documents and the personal drive to create an individually expressive style that underlay many of the greatest achievements in the rising practice of calligraphy over the centuries that followed.

The example in fig. 5.13 reproduces a rubbing of an inscription on stone, which was engraved after a particular example – or perhaps a copy of a particular example – of Zhong You's writing. Although once written on silk or paper, much of today's canon of early regular script (and other writing styles) is based on reproductions in stone. Some of these stones were even cut on the basis of rubbings taken from earlier stone monuments that had been lost or destroyed. Thus, although many early calligraphers' talents are not in doubt, credit for the evidence of their art must go to generations of skilled yet nameless stonemasons and the enthusiasts who took rubbings of their work.

Even specimens of regular script and running script by Wang Xizhi (AD 307–65), the most celebrated name in Chinese calligraphy, have survived only through successive transfers between paper and stone. Works transmitted in this manner have nevertheless been revered as the loftiest models of writing style.

The achievements of Zhong You and Wang Xizhi in regular script remained a minority taste for at least a century after Wang's death. Most documents during this period seem to have been written in clerical script or one of the cursive scripts. Only in the fifth century did regular script begin to displace the pre-eminence of clerical script. Ironically, considering the later dominance of regular script as a medium for some of the most confident expressions of Chinese cultural identity ever written, this change developed fastest among the predominantly Turkic regimes of north China during the fragmented period of the Northern and Southern Dynasties (AD 420–581). But in 581, following four centuries of disunity, these same regimes' social and political structures provided the strong underpinnings for a new imperial unity. Regular script was retained as the standard form of writing for government documents, monumental inscriptions and religious dedications. The surviving specimens of Wang Xizhi's writing were decreed the highest exemplars of style and promulgated as the official canon. Lengthy works such as dynastic histories (fig. 5.14), for instance, were copied in this script by the most skilled hands in keeping with the high status reserved for historiography.

Fig. 5.14 Section from a 9th-century copy of the *Zhoushu* [History of the Northern Zhou Dynasty] (AD 559–81), paper, copyist unknown, private collection, Japan. After Nakata Yūjirō, ed., *Tō shōhon*, Osaka, 1981: no. 59.

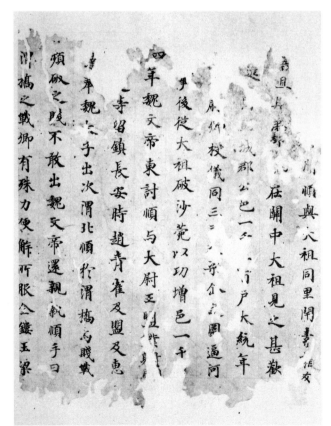

Regular script establishes strict rules for the exact order in which the constituent strokes of a character should be written. Strokes consist of horizontals, verticals, diagonals, dots, hooks and several other simple line forms. These are written in specific sequences. For example, when a character – or part of a character – combines horizontal and vertical lines, the former are written ahead of the latter. Invariably, writing a character begins with the upper strokes. To enclose elements within a surrounding border, the three upper sides of the border are drawn first with two strokes. After that, the inner elements are added, and only then is the fourth side drawn across the base. This is the sequence for writing the character *gu* 'firm':

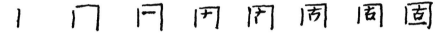

gu 'firm' (showing stroke order in eight stages)

These rules for sequence are often detectable in the directions of a writer's brushwork. They also provide the obvious conventions that artists broke in their most skilful executions of cursive style. It is probably no coincidence that as successive generations of the Tang elite undertook the first truly comprehensive standardization of regular script, some among their number created what have remained unparalleled achievements in cursive writing. The most famous of these writers was the Buddhist monk Huai Su (*c.* 735–*c.* 799). A self-introduction (fig. 5.15) that he wrote in AD 777 comprises a paper scroll over seven metres long. Its characters are an extraordinary production of speed and control. Huai Su's

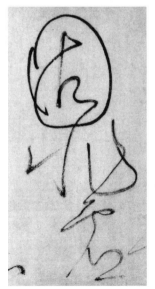

Fig. 5.15 Detail from Huai Su (*c.* 735–*c.* 799), *zixu tie* 'letter of self-introduction', AD 777, 28.3 x 75 cm, National Palace Museum, Taipei. After Wen C. Fong and James C. Y. Watt, *Possessing the Past: Treasures from the National Palace Museum*, New York/Taipei, 1996: pl. 56.

execution of the character *gu* 'firm' uses two strokes of the brush. The first stroke is a short downward hook comprising the left edge of the enclosure, and the second writes the rest of the character. Most obviously, it flouts the conventions of regular script by sealing the enclosure before completing the inner strokes. In fact, the second stroke only terminates as a vertical element in the following character.

Despite its advance under the Tang, regular script did not dominate all spheres of textual production. For instance, it was only under later governments that mints completely abandoned using seal-script legends on coinage. When at last they did, regular-script inscriptions appeared in thoroughly personal styles. One of the last issues of the Northern Song (960–1127) bears the writing of Emperor Huizong, whose distinctive calligraphy, highly acclaimed during his culturally brilliant reign, was frequently copied or forged (fig. 5.16).

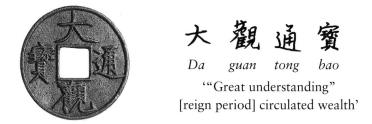

大 觀 通 寶
Da   guan   tong   bao
'"Great understanding"
[reign period] circulated wealth'

Fig. 5.16 Bronze coin inscribed *Da guan tong bao* 'Wealth circulated [in the reign period of] Great Understanding', first issued AD 1107, D. 4 cm, BM (CM) CH 730.

Printed books, whose beginnings date to the ninth century or perhaps earlier, adopted regular script for block printing and later for movable type. Even if printed books – any books – were available to far fewer people than is often claimed, the role that printing played in spreading and maintaining orthographic standards throughout imperial China – and Korea and Japan – cannot be exaggerated. Printing was probably the fundamental reason why no other new script form ever overshadowed regular script. Today, all over the Chinese world, regular script is the style adopted to teach literacy, to print most publications and to appear on computer screens.

Modern simplifications

During the twentieth century, in order to promote a higher level of national literacy, the government in mainland China supervised a programme of reducing the complexity of the most common characters. Acquiring literacy in the Chinese writing system certainly takes longer than it does for an alphabetic system, so simplified characters were promulgated in 1955, 1964 and 1977. The last batch was criticized as representing an oversimplification: no longer was it easy to distinguish between a familiar prototype and what could appear as a totally new character. This batch was withdrawn within the same year.

Many of the simplified characters put into circulation in 1955 and 1964 were simplifications or cursive shorthand forms invented many centuries earlier. The multiple strokes of denser forms were collapsed into more sparing combinations that retained something of their prototypes' familiar appearance. The nine strokes used to write the character *shu*, which stands for the verb 'to write' and for the noun 'book', were simplified to a total of four. *Ma* 'horse' was reduced from ten strokes to three. Many characters contain simplified determinatives, such as the speech determinative in *qi* 'to deceive', simplified from seven strokes to two:

書　　书　　*shu* 'to write', 'book'

馬　　马　　*ma* 'horse'

謀　　谋　　*qi* 'to deceive'

Official publishing now uses a prescribed number of simplified characters, but many more appear in less controlled circumstances (fig. 5.17).

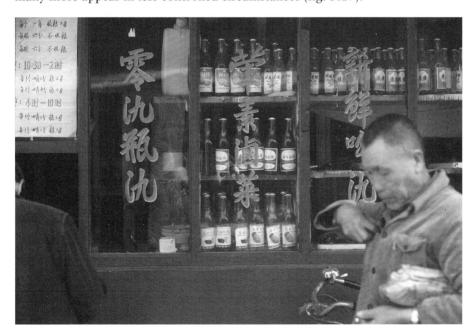

Fig. 5.17 Shopfront in south-west China (author's photograph).

One of the characters used three times on this shopfront is *jiu* 'alcohol'. Its full form of ten strokes has been simplified to five and then still further reduced by writing the three left-hand dots as a single stroke.

酒   沈

This simplification follows the principles of creating characters described throughout this book. That is, a determinative for the character's meaning – in this example the three dots of 'water' for words associated with liquids – is combined with a phonetic element. The simplified phonetic in this character is *jiu* 'nine'. The two words *jiu* 'alcohol' and 'nine' are both third-tone pronunciations in SMC. Not only graphic simplifications but many new words are created in this way, offering significant testimony that Chinese writing is sufficiently versatile to write words that do not exist in SMC, to create non-official abbreviations and to transliterate foreign words into Chinese characters.

6
The Endurance of Chinese Writing

Chinese writing today still uses characters. Writing with logograms was preferred to adopting an absolutely phonetic writing system. This preference even dominated the adapted uses of Chinese characters by neighbouring writing systems.

Some of the examples provided in this book show instances of phonetic borrowing that prove how writers in early China often created characters which represented primarily the sounds for the words they wished to express. Frequently two writers wrote two dissimilar characters for the same word. Had this development continued unabated, Chinese writing might have become a system denoting only the sounds of the language, without providing a distinct character – a logogram – for every word. Writing with a phonetic syllabary might have evolved in early China as it was destined to do in Japan half a millennium later. A syllabary is a system that uses one sign per syllable. For example, the Japanese word *kujira* can be broken down into the three syllables *ku-ji-ra*, each of which is written with a single sign, often referred to as a syllabogram:

kujira 'whale'

More will be said about this Japanese system below.

Japanese, however, is a polysyllabic language, and the high number of syllables in many Japanese words radically limits the instances of two words sounding exactly the same. This is different from Chinese. Nevertheless, as William Boltz has argued, a polysyllabic tendency in Chinese was apparent prior to the Qin unification in the third century BC. This is demonstrated in the *Shuowen jiezi* of AD 100, in which Xu Shen, observing the conditions of several regional languages, noted several disyllabic words which he recorded with one character for each syllable. Had it been a priority to record the disyllabic vocabulary spoken in different regions of his day, he could have listed many more. As it was, his notes were not intended to provide alternatives to the prescribed monosyllabic forms in the main text of his dictionary. Some words, however, existed only as disyllables and possessed no monosyllabic alternative with which to suppress them. Even though these polysyllabic words could have been written by pure phonetic borrowing, with only the smallest chance of confusion with other disyllables of the same values, the practice was to avoid doing this. The phonetic representatives of each portion of a disyllabic word were always consigned an appropriate determinative. For instance:

hudie
'butterfly'

Both syllables possess an 'insect' determinative even though it would have been – and still would be – quite possible to abandon these extra clarifiers and to use the word's two phonetic components, *hu* and *die*, as a disyllabic item unambiguously representing the word for butterfly. Had this abandonment actually occurred, the appearance of the word 'butterfly' would have amounted to an instance of syllabographic writing. But the habit of adding determinatives to phonetic signs weakened the potential for syllabographic development and strengthened the supremacy of a determinative-based system. And these trends were directly antithetical to any tendency towards phonetic writing by means of the desemanticized signs which comprise a syllabary or an alphabet.

The Qin government implemented its reform of the Chinese script against this background, aiming to promulgate common standards for thousands of Chinese words. This was a daunting task. Early Han texts of the second century BC, recently excavated in southern China, include characters written in both the Qin-prescribed form and the previously current Chu form, which the former was meant to have replaced. Clearly, scribes in the south struggled for a long time to follow the new writing rules prescribed by the central government in the north.

Writing other languages
Finally, throughout a long history, the function of Chinese characters did not develop exclusively within the confines of Chinese civilization. Their entry into the writing of first Japanese and later Vietnamese illustrates two distinct yet significant historical episodes.

The Chinese principle of combining sound and meaning in one logogram once functioned to write Vietnamese. In the thirteenth century a system was devised for writing the sounds of Vietnamese speech with the closest adaptable rhymes from literary Chinese. Borrowing Chinese phonetic components, the Vietnamese creators of Chû'nôm ('Southern script') assigned new determinatives to the phonetic borrowings they had selected. For instance, for the Vietnamese verb *an* 'to eat', they took the Chinese character *an* 'peace' and added the 'mouth' determinative to the left:

an 'peace'

Vietnamese *an* 'to eat'

The chief drawback of this system was that it presupposed the reader and writer of Chû'nôm was literate in Chinese. Still, it was a viable method and gave rise to some remarkable results, ranging from monuments in stone to romantic literature. Its reliance on the sounds of a second language, however, doomed its long-term survival. The European introduction of the Roman alphabet during the seventeenth century provided a system that reduced the problem of borrowing to a much more manageable scale. A modified Roman alphabet was adopted as the official Vietnamese script in 1910.

An utterly different adaptation had occurred long before in Japan. Japanese is a polysyllabic language quite unrelated to the grammatical or syntactical structures of Chinese. But, because it borrowed the Chinese writing system, its relationship to the sounds of Chinese is both intimate and complicated. Its vocabulary contains many imported Chinese words. In certain conditions these are pronounced in the Japanese equivalent of the Chinese pronunciation of several centuries ago – when the characters first entered Japanese circulation. For instance, the character for Chinese *shan* ('mountain') can be read in Japan as *san*, which is recognizably close to a Chinese pronunciation even today, or as *yama*, which is the native Japanese pronunciation.

Until the advent of Chinese characters there was no system for writing down Japanese pronunciation, or for recording the individual syllables of Japanese words. A fascinating solution to this problem was the use of one Chinese character for each syllable of a Japanese word. Late-seventh-century wood tablets (*mokkan*) from the site of the capital at Fujiwara contain such formations as:

ika 'cuttlefish'

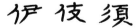

igisu 'seaweed'

The characters here represent Japanese renderings of Chinese sounds, and they were chosen irrespective of their meaning in Chinese. They can be called syllabograms since, unlike logograms that represent whole words, they record syllables. The final development of such a process was to create a syllabary. Early in the eighth century writers started to use the *hiragana* system of writing Japanese words, in which a fixed group of syllabograms derived from Chinese characters (totalling just under fifty signs) functioned to write all the sounds of Japanese words. (A second syllabary, *katakana*, using modified forms of the *hiragana*, was later developed to write foreign words.) The following are four examples of Chinese characters and their Japanese reductions as signs in the *hiragana* system of phonetic notation:

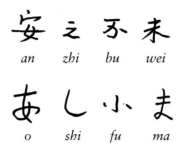

These signs are interspersed with the full forms of Chinese characters:

'The aeroplane took off'

飛行機は出発した。

The same sentence can also be written entirely with *hiragana*:

ひこうきはしゅっぱつした。

The Japanese adaptation of Chinese characters illustrates precisely the direction in which Chinese writing never developed. In China, systematic use of determinatives offered instead a method that diverged sharply from both a phonetic syllabary and an alphabet, and maintained the primacy of logograms.

That writing in China did not evolve towards a desemanticized syllabo-graphic system does not represent a failure. Logographic writing offered many advantages in the specific linguistic conditions of China, supporting the cultural priority of reading what had been written in the past, creating a distinctive literature and engendering perhaps the world's richest and most sophisticated tradition of writing as an art form. Not least, its writing system enabled the far-flung administration of successive governments to function, and it remains an essential ingredient in the unity of China today.

Further Reading

Boltz, William, *The Origin and Early Development of the Chinese Writing System*, New Haven, 1994

Bottéro, Françoise, *Sémantisme et classification dans l'écriture chinoise: les systèmes de classement des caractères par clés du* Shuowen jiezi *au* Kangxi zidian, Paris, 1996

Bright, William, and Daniels, Peter, *The World's Writing Systems*, Oxford/New York, 1996

Chen Mengjia, 'Xi Zhou tongqi duandai', part 3, *Kaogu xuebao*, 1956.1: 65–114

DeFrancis, John, *The Chinese Language: Fact and Fantasy*, Honolulu, 1984

Diringer, David, *The Alphabet: A Key to the History of Mankind*, London/New York, 1947

Dong Chuping, *Wu Yue Xu Shu jinwen jishi*, Hangzhou, 1992

Duan Yucai (1735–1815), *Shuowen jiezi zhu*, Shanghai, 1988

Gao Ming, *Zhongguo guwenzixue tonglun*, Beijing, 1987

Gelb, I. J., *A Study of Writing*, Chicago, 1952

Harris, Roy, *The Origin of Writing*, London, 1986

Keightley, David N., *Sources of Shang History: The Oracle-bone Inscriptions of Bronze Age China*, Berkeley/Los Angeles, 1978

Ledderose, Lothar, *Mi Fu and the Classical Tradition of Chinese Calligraphy*, Princeton, NJ, 1979

Li Ji, *Anyang*, Seattle/London, 1977

Nguyên Dình Hoà, 'Chu'Nôm: The Demotic System of Writing in Vietnam', *Journal of the American Oriental Society*, 79/4 (1959): 270–4

Norman, Jerry, *Chinese*, Cambridge, 1988

Qiu Xigui, 'On the Method of Studying Ancient Chinese Script' (trans. Gilbert Mattos), *Early China*, 11–12 (1985–7): 301–16

Qiu Xigui, *Wenzixue gaiyao*, Beijing, 1988

Robinson, Andrew, *The Story of Writing: Alphabets, Hieroglyphs and Pictograms*, London, 1995

Schlombs, Adele, *Huai-su and the Beginnings of Wild Cursive Script in Chinese Calligraphy*, Stuttgart, 1998

Seely, Christopher, *A History of Writing in Japan*, Leiden, 1991

Shaughnessy, Edward L., *Sources of Western Zhou History: Inscribed Bronze Vessels*, Berkeley/Los Angeles, 1991

Shaughnessy, Edward L., *New Sources of Early Chinese History: An Introduction to the Reading of Inscriptions and Manuscripts*, Berkeley, 1997

Shima Kunio, *Inkyo bokuji sōrui*, Tokyo, 1967

Shirakawa Shizuka, *Kimbun tsūshaku*, no. 11, published as *Hakutsuru Bijutsukan shi*, vol. 11 (1965)

Shirakawa Shizuka, *Jitō*, Tokyo, 1984

Tang Lan, *Xi Zhou qingtongqi mingwen fendai shizheng*, Beijing, 1986

Tsien, Tsuen-hsuin, *Written on Bamboo and Silk*, Chicago, 1962

Tung Tso-pin, *Fifty Years of Studies in Oracle Inscriptions*, Tokyo, 1964

Sources for ancient forms of character used in this book

Chen Peifen, *Shanghai Bowuguan: Zhongguo gudai qingtongqi*, London, 1995

Kobayashi Hiroshi, *Kodai kanji iken*, Tokyo, 1977

Ma Chengyuan et al., eds, *Shang Zhou qingtongqi ji mingwen xuan*, vol. 4, Beijing, 1990

Wang Baoming, ed., *Zhongguo xingcao shufa dazidian*, Beijing, 1992

Zhang Shouzhong, *Zhongshan wang Cuo qi wenzi bian*, Beijing, 1981

Zhang Shouzhong, *Shuihudi Qin jian wenzi bian*, Beijing, 1994

Index